DIFFERE... SECONDS 2

MW00928062

HELLO, FRIEND—SEE, HEAR, FEEL THE DIFFERENCE

R. S. APPLE

To: Ryan an Julia J.

I havent Known you two that long,
but you seem pretty cool to me. Thanks
for wishing me a Happy Birthday yesterday,
meant alot! I hope you both enjoy
these two books Different Seconds and
Different Seconds 2. :)

R. S. Apple

Sunday July 27, 2014,

iUniverse LLC
Bloomington

DIFFERENT SECONDS 2
Hello, Friend—See, Hear, Feel the Difference

iUniverse books may be ordered through booksellers or by contacting:

iUniverse LLC
1663 Liberty Drive
Bloomington, IN 47403
www.iuniverse.com
1-800-Authors (1-800-288-4677)

ISBN: 978-1-4917-2911-3 (sc)
ISBN: 978-1-4917-2910-6 (e)

Library of Congress Control Number: 2014905854

Printed in the United States of America.

iUniverse rev. date: 04/08/2014

INTRODUCTION

Hello again my friends and followers, welcome to the new an second book of the Different Seconds saga! This time around the styles an themes have changed, more in depth, more poems, more imagination. Take a ride from out of this world, near to armageddon, back to real life and across the stars towards the heaven. My name is R. S. Apple for those of you who don't know me, I live in Southern Ontario, in a town called Orillia near the Muskoka region. I have been writing poetry for about 8 years now. Please enjoy this new collection of poems as I take your imagination to wild worlds and extraordinary places!

Lost Sheep

What bases anything
You write for people
You work for people
You try to impress people

Still the word doesn't make it through
Trying your best sometimes does not work
Giving your all
And for what

Bah, Bah, Bah
Goes the lonely sheep
No matter what it does
It feels like it can't win

People try to feed it
Wanting it to go away and leave
How hard is it to push people away
To some its not hard at all

Can you feel this world starting to fall
Lots a fish in the sea
Seems like a load of sheep to me
Proper bait can't be found

Bah, Bah, Bah
Goes the lonely sheep
No worries
That sheep is only me . . .

Friday, December 8, 2006.

Your You

Standing for many things
In this life
All of us persons
Each stand for something different

Looking under earths clouds
Above the Oceans
On the ground
Where the streets meet the sand

What's in this planets pocket
That you might stand for
Love of a soul mate
Feeling connected just like a truck and trailer

Cheering for a team
Education your trying to achieve
Religious figures that believe in you
Asking constant questions of where to go

Standing for freedom of speaking the mind
Remembering a past soul that has dropped
Trying to stop threats to the nature and person
Or just to try find ones self

We all stand under the same star
Surrounded by blue liquids and ceilings
Eyes by other air breathers
Rising towers of steel and cement

We stand for times existence
We stand for others
Whatever interest you have
Is what stands for your you . . . .

September, Sunday 9, 2007.

Dawn of a New Sky

Ever step on a land
Where the sun meets the ground
When it comes down
It brings the darkness with it

Blue sky turns to a black canvas
Warm air becomes a chilly reminder of things to come
A dry ground is now being damped
Another world starts to take over

Colours of the fall trees
Can no longer be seen
Wide open fields of dried up corn stems
Are vanished with the blackened sky

Motorized carriages are trying to out run the other sky
No matter how fast they go
This darkness always overcomes
All surrounding area

With the coming of the new sky
Is one where eight legged lives
Try to capture there food source
A game they better win, to see a new sun

Blinded wings also come out now
Looking for there pry
Pry looking pry
So they can survive another night

In the ceiling above
Shiny crystals are beaming down
To the ground that lays under them
People on the ground, looking up at them

Seasons are now changing
As one sky becomes more then the other
The air that's breathed is only made colder
No matter what sky is looking down

Certain creatures start fading off
Landscapes well soon be covered
A country is going to be transformed
As it might feel

Just as things are beginning to feel forever
A golden amber comes up from under the ground
Colours, fields, comfortable air is now reborn
A favourite sky has come back
But a season soon to change regardless.

September, Monday 24, 2007.

Feeling of Novem

The winds of November
Have proceeded once again
Trees are bare
And reaching for the Heavens

A sky so dark
Appears as the final curtain
The last skit
In a season of Winter

Not a single soul insight
Feels like this world is my own
A feeling of alone
Not something unknown

Night lamps
Shining on the black coloured water
Fish swim away
And get less then hotter

Temperature can't be touched
Skin numb from bold cold
Warmth can be found
In gas powered houses

A section of weeks
That holds no one promise
Dimmered sense of place
Have an urge to pack a suitcase

Lights behind the final curtain
Are becoming brighter
Begins the last quarter of the show
Keep your feet on the floor
Maintain yourself with the flow

Friday, November 2, 2007.

Urabf Saayah Shtin Risnda

Street lights shining out full
On the street I am standing on
Look like stars they do
Making this place seem special

Shutting my eyes
I can feel and see another wonderland
People smiling
Having so much fun is being shown

In a bar
On the beach
At the mall
Cruising the streets of magic

Experiencing a happy feeling
Walking heavens clouds
Owning the world
I feel like I do

Friends make me feel so special
Like something I've never been
One with everyone
And belonging

In a trance that I never want to leave
This soul won't let the feeling go
Greatness is plentiful
So is my heart and mind

As the flow pushes forward
I will remain happy and strong
Re-opening my eyes
Remembering where I am

Still inside remaining bright
Rain pours all around
While waiting for my ride
To futures night

A truck pulls up to me
Just before I climb in
Feel the past once more with my soul
Giving me this positive power
Friends from past our still now
Thanks to them I say
From now until my last day
They helped push the negative away!

Saturday, December 6th, 2007.

Province Four Random, Odd Occurrences

Why have we found the reasons to live?
As the water goes drip, drip, drip
Watch a kid lose his lid
Thinking about something hard, to find out it's what you did

Rhyme or reason
Winter is the hard cold season
Rap your best friend's birthday gift with a ribbon
Pitching in to buy booze, dips in

Lips are leaking
Ceils are breaking
People are always mistaking
Shadows of the night are soul taking

Glass window on cement ledge
In truths of court reciting a pledge
Huge cutting scissors for town hall hedge
Fries from the chip truck all seem to have a wedge

Mosquito's biting
Gangs in country or city fighting
Tall poles lighting
Look at dark sky, watch the lightning

Many car crash victims
Dealing with a cancer patients symptoms
Cooking dinner in your friends kitchen
Seems like many people are bitchin

Dope, other drugs, fish
Would it kill you to clean this dish?
Girl you have a crush on named Trish
Don't act like a son of a bitch

Under sun getting burned tan
Toronto Maple Leafs, not a fan
Elephant running, made me ran
If you believe in something take a stand

Avoid the king of a jungle
Over two thousand piece's to this puzzle
Feeling loved getting snuggled
Be careful of stranger cause they'll

Out breaking wild fires
Exploding rubber tires
Wild tuna getting caught in net wires
Eating hot dogs would you choose Oscar Mayer?

Mustard, ketchup, cooking oil
Lawn mower not starting, cause of jammed coil
Spending a week in a castle feeling royal
No other words rhyme, feed your car oil

Hot humid summer brings severe wicked weather
Killing a cow for coat made of leather
Mind over matter, your fake like pleather
To drunk from that night, do you remember?

Driving, flying to faraway places
Some how forgetting to pack suitcases
Enjoy your trip, next time tie them shoe laces
Some international food just tasteless

Red fifty dollar bill
Vehicle under powered fails to make hill
Finding out your allergic to daffodils
Wishing you remembered to take the pill

Spray amazing smelling Axe
Paying every witch way lots of tax
Sucking on orange frosters from Max
Just a random poem, sit down and relax.

Friday, July 18, 2008.

Finding the Christmas Star

It is written somewhere
Writings that speak of a Christmas Star
They speak of the ones who are lost
And trying to find there way home

On an early ending winter fishing trip
Right before the dawn of Christmas
Three brothers are beginning their journey home
All thrilled to see their own families and friends

Crossing the frozen waterway
Is the only single passage to their destination
Two of them hop on an ATV
The third also the youngest rides the sleigh behind

Its dark
All that can be seen
Is the moon lit snowscape
Unlike the pressure crack just ahead

The oldest slams on the break
But in most situations
Like this, its to late
Open water under the crack

Blue liquid rises from above
Takes all down
Except the youngest brother
He's left with freezing skin and a shattered mind

Feels like hours go by
Actual only minutes
A bright star in the sky
Appears to be descending

The brother thinks possible helicopter
Once the so called star lands
It takes shape of a ghostly figure
This faded soul walks toward the down brother

And speaks into his ear
Stay focused
You can embrace the pain and make it
Or the pain can be taken away

Lights of snowmobiles
As well as other rescue crafts
Can be seen coming from shore
Just a little longer says the mysterious voice

The young one only wants one answer
Where are my brothers?
As the figure walks away
They found the Christmas Star   Mon, Dec 24, 2007.

Worlds

Up in the sky
High and mighty like a bird
Scanning oceans of beauty
Inhailing clouds of moisture

Viewing urban centers reaching across the lands
Rivers and lakes cutting there shapes out
Trees trying to touch the clouds
Flowers stretching for the sun

Small lives trying to find there way
Find there purpose
Innocent in this vast globe
Futures can't be known

Clouds draping towards the surface
Liquid droplets tapping hands
Electric bolts stabbing the ground
And keep coming around

Gills passing through water
Creatures come from sky to find they're needed
Logs of life die, then fall
Much like Berlin Wall

This water table
Has many worlds locked within
Mystery's to be seen
Through that can in the recycle bin

Saturday, December 29, 2007.

Broken television with that coat hanger antenna
Washing your mouth out with Scope, cause your toothpaste seems defective
Trying to feed a Zebra at the zoo peanuts, and finding out how sharp those teeth are
Using selective hearing on purpose to ignore your wife, so you can watch that dvd movie

Hey, look over in this corner
Didn't expect to see writing over here did you?
Confused? I know you are, it will only get more complicated as we move forward
WHAT! You have some questions? Sorry you'll have to wait until the end.

Mother and law coming over for the weekend, sun or rain the bitch will drive you insane
Half melted snowman in the front yard, bent over, looks like its trying to find something
Poison ivy all over your body, itch, scratch, burn
Sunshine rainbow towering across the forever country side

Have you figured it out yet, what we are talking about?
Sorry did you say, you wanted a hint?
Wow, sorry friend I cannot tell you yet
Keep on reading though, it might jump out and hit you in the face or sensitive area

Purchasing a new roof over your head in a already jam, crammed neighborhood
It seemed like a good idea at time, doesn't cut it, when the rest of time comes around
Dreaming of where you might meet your next girlfriend or boyfriend
Power outages in the dark, cause mass panic for individuals afraid of the night

I hear your brain thinking and wondering where this is going
Words will start to get more intense and fast paced
Hey, don't be sacred, there just letters forming words
They can't hurt you, but it might make you think your in the writings

Explosion over your head, glass shattering all around, the ball now in the living room
Face, racing, blood pumping, acceleration, zigzagging through still traffic
Shaking, vibration, being tossed like bobble head doll,
turbulence, steal crushing nightmare
Tornados from above, breathing winds from devil lungs, destruction, life levelled

Stop shaking friend, your back on solid ground now
Ever think about where your life is headed?
Some people believe that experiences from the past, make us who we will be in the future
They could be right, but I don't know.

Laying on a strip of sand, letting the sun drink your skin
Binge booze drinking, staggering all over the property, hangover of pain follows suit
Three and a half inch floppy, star bucks coffee, thick
maple toffee, huge waves make a boat rocky
Unemployed bagging for hard earned money, lazy jerks this ain't funny

Oh my god, were talking about a game
No, not like basketball, or hockey, think bigger friend
Doesn't matter, cause were at the end of this writing
Friend, were talking about life, a journey of everyday
occurrences. Let me be the first to welcome you too

WILD GAME

Saturday, August 16, 2008.

License Plate to Zero

Endurance
Mark men's ship
Personal traits
That each of us possesses

Secret ideas
Hidden concepts
Mysterious outlooks
Of past, present and future

Social values
Individual status
Underground stance
Just a little water well help that plant

Plastic bottles
Metal cans
Wooden boxes
That prevent food bands

Rich places
Sad faces
Over priced product
One to many audits

Flooded continents
Over populated lands
War, conflict and death
History repeats itself with man

Canada big
New Zealand small
United States
Wants to bully with us all

Powerful thinkers
Afraid followers
High maintained persons
In the gutter being a stoner

Two sides to every mirror
Many statements of thought
We all live on this planet
Is it possible to get along or not?

Tuesday, January 1, 2008.

Greed, For Uncertainty

Whether you're on some far away land
On top of the North Pole
Where water may have been
Now nothing but sand

Once crop lands
Pavement strips with electric flow
Where instead of days
Well only take you an hour or so

Loss of jobs
Loss of life
Money has keys into everything
Except the unforgiving night

Snow falls
Once where grass was known
Oil floods out of grounds
Where buffalo use to rome

Forests for decks
Sheep for shirts
Fossils for fuels
Lives held for ransom

Addiction to gambling
Sitting instead of standing
Drive thru for coffee beans
Ships sinking and not landing

Cutting corners to win the race
Saving a buck being a cheap skate
Hit and run and just driving away
Ignoring all warning signs

Extinction of wildlife
Over populated planet
Warming of breeze
Using a million Kleenex's for one sneeze
Your already awake this is not a dream . . . .

Sunday, January 27, 2008.

Downtown Streets

Breathing hard
Don't know if he can be saved
Eyes opening and closing
In state of shock

Stay with me your going to be fine
Just hold on a few more ticks
Ambulance is nearing
Senseless act of another individual

Flashing lights pull up to the curb
Paramedics assist
But could it be to late
No one likes fate

Air is cold
Sky pitch dark
I'm being told
He was given the mark

Racing through bloody streets
Lights of red can't slow it down
Looking for stars
So I can pray that this life is found

Seconds turn into minutes
Minutes turn into breaths
Park up against emergency doors
Bed on wheels hit's the floor

Souls dressed in white
Attempt to save this life
Wave goodbye
Not knowing if he'll be seen again

Stand outside
In fresh cold air
Waiting for the sun or response
Sounds seem silent

Answers seem bleak
We failed, but tried
Another innocent life
Taken this week

Nothing to do but follow the coffin
Shed tears of piece
Lay this young life to rest
And try to prevent any further unrest . . . .

Saturday, February 22, 2008.

Lost Distance

A shooting star stretching across the heavens
Walking on a thin strip of beach with waves at my feet
Air of warmth kissing my face
Can't trip over these feet no shoe or lace

Sand creeping between ten different toes
Listening to an iPod and trying to get low
Laughing like a child
Before the now existing time

Remembering sweet eyes and faces
Wishing I could be in those warm loving places
This mind rolling across earth's table like dice
Like cutting a wire trying to splice

Voices of angels still can be herd in these drums
Forever standing waiting for these angels to come
From the North a light up high above can be seen
Closing eyes a couple of times, to be not a dream

Fly's of glow buzz around in adjacent fields
No sounds of any kind not even from traveling wheels
Thinking of just memories
Wishing of leaving please

Hoping to find another soul walking this beach
No lines of modern communication and I cannot be reached
Strolling on the path of apparent far from no end
Heart made of steel unlike plastic that can bend

Chance of not being found
Gives this smile a frown
Shooting star still stretching for heavens door
Now time to kneel on this sandy floor

Happier occurrences currently being thought of
A white bird lands in front, the species a dove
Sign of better weather in my forecast
Sound of a rescue helicopter at last

Sunday, March 2, 2008.

20

The
Forgotten

Green canvas surrounds above us
A thick pine needle floor under our feet
Cool fresh breeze from rocky temples near by
Sound of flowing shallow waters beside my ear

Predators screaming trying to intimidate fear
Looking far off to the distance, could be deer
Signs from the black bear beast
Suggests they could be near

Pitch a tent under the next telephone poll
Forbid a storm forms, cause this stump to fall
Meals are not found in cans
Only way to survive is to feed yourself from the land

Golden amber starts down for home
Soon the sky will become dark and me alone
Black tarp twinkles aloud
Trying to remain silent, so I can stay alive and proud

Noises of breath and walk are heard all around
Only one expression on my face, forms a frown
Cold winter like air invades my primitive roof
Wishing the amber would come from above soon

Like melted butter on toast, frost floods the ground
Morning rays cause this land to shine like diamonds
So the cycle starts another round
I am still out here, lost and not found

Sunday, March 16, 2008.

Twenty
Below

We found her on empty city streets
Looking for food in dumpsters
No money of any
Much value in penny's

Pavement for flooring
Used cardboard for an overhang
A stranger offers the dollars of five
Another night she can remain alive

Not overly far away
An older gentleman is trying to find cans
Sounds disgusting and unsanitary
One nights work can make him feel wealthy

They want to trade cold for heat
So feeling comes back to there feet
Warmth is like love
Cold shits on you like a dove

Age of eighteen already trying to sell her body
Some with green will do anything to cause naughty
Illegal crime just to earn few dimes
Drugs other forms of abuse apparently gives some the excuse

Some are not privileged with even clothes
These individuals get tossed into the cold
Not given a purpose or soul
Seems like we all say no

Lack of hope and no chances
Left behind and given no advances
Under valued and lost
Pull some change out of the pocket and toss

Wednesday, March 26, 2008.

Don't Want to Say
Goodbye

Certain days we lose
Some special nights we win
Attracted to soul and heart
They see us as who we are, and where we have been

Beach a boat on a shoal
Back your new truck into a pole
Not stopping at the gate
And driving straight through the toll

Try to jump the lake on your bike
Smoking up feeling higher then your kite
Friends laugh, cause your pants look to tight
Knowing when to step in and end the fight

Drinking to the point of passing out
You drove the wrong way on a European round about
Broke your leg snowboarding, trying not to pout
Not getting the girl you wanted and striking out

Setting fire to a tree
Your best friend dying on the sidewalk from to much ecstasy
Park in the wrong spot, pay the fee
Kicking around a not so lively nest, still got stung by that bee

Up all night finishing your work
Your roommates being an annoying and thinking they're jerks
Thinking your all that and getting hurt
Puffing a magic sensation and feeling the ultimate perk

Presenting drunk
Laundry not done for days, smelling like a skunk
Causing unnecessary problems, being a punk
Trying to shove many nuts in your mouth, acting like a chipmunk

Getting better then normal grades
Instead of the ace of diamonds, you're the ace of spades
Graduation time, feeling free, feeling made
OSAP wants your future pay

Times are what defy life
Many moments with chills
Feeling sometimes life goes down hill
Experience of College a one of kind thrill

Wednesday, April 16, 2008.

Floating along a roadway in stand still stance
Looking for much direction
Also looking for mystical chance
A way to find our final destination

Seagulls flying overhead in a slow hazy motion
Orange steal with black lettering warning of delays ahead
In distance bright red coloured plastic signals the stop
Sun shining down baking all who travel on rubber tracks

                    Were walking towards you in the future
                  Try stopping us, its already been foreseen
                        Fish travel the tropic circle
                            In search for food
                        In search of mates and fate

                          Welcome back, you have returned for another round
                                      Get rid of those shoes and sit down
                                              Questions already?
                                        Holy friend keep it steady

                  Glass bottom boat hard to keep afloat
                  Light up fire to smoke your toke

Reindeer walk up to roadside
Freezing slow still in vision of strong head lamps
Can't keep pace with quick low witted drivers
Black and white at speed of flight well tackle the troubles

                              All over this page confusing that mind of yours
                                          Can't help but continue
                                  Not trying to tick you off friend
                              Getting you to think until the end

                    Verge of going insane
                  Purely missing with your brain
                    Headaches and pains
                    Just can't to go away

                                                        Right
Left

                    Center
                              This writing is turning into a blender

Mislead feeling like your lost

Trying to prove a point to a friends boss
Feeling of broken an unwanted

Welcome to **Tunnel Vision** friend
Where the writing is completely tossed

Thursday, August 21, 2008.

Covered by Night

Hiding behind shadows on 5th and main
Is an individual that had much to say
Waiting for a particular time
To let his voice be heard

Many have denied him free speech
They say he couldn't measure up to more then a rat finding cheese
He don't need your pity or concern
Figured out ways to prove the non believers

During the sunshine reign
Nicest guy in the world
Help the closest out when there in need
Known as the living saint

A mind changes according to the flavour of hour
Stopping this occurrence is only a thought, can't be done
Goes home gets ready for a night of intensions
Who ever has crossed him will soon regret these decisions

Grabs the keys to black tinted windows SUV machine
Loaded with big barrels that can shot aluminum rounds
The world of the underground only knows him as the devils player
Few in the streets have any courage of challenging this soul

Who's on the list tonight?
An enemy or a stranger
Ones that only have to fear
Low lives robbing from his soul or the innocent

Quiet night streets can be shattered by the sound of the loud engine suburban
Paved of black with lines of yellow and white could become red
Ones who serve and protect believe him to be the power of myths and legends
Someone who knows things before they happen, or can see what will happen

First target of the night located in near by sight
Sniper shot to easy
Drive by shine off much more sleazy
Enemy never saw it coming

Views of the world see him as both as a protector that fears no one
And someone who has the damned soul
No matter the theory that's laid upon him
One's with futures in crime
He will make sure they live that afterlife in hells damned sin

The Devils Player is Steve Wimm. Life with heavenly sins

Monday, May 2, 2008.

Roadway of Air

Break down on the highway
Bad times being thrown in your direction
Under paying job
Any money, is thought to be good

Blind date to start on the Blvd.
Once again stood up
This same heart being ripped apart
How many instances do there have to be?

Spend hours along riverside
Trying to catch a fish and maybe a thought
What's reserved in the future
Probably should of picked better bait and spot

Sound of the wind coming from high above
Tall trees swinging to the beat of motion
Birds struggling against the invisible current
Debris from motorists flying all around

Ducks swimming with ducklings
Moms and dads playing with their little ones
Many stories have just begun
With smiles of fun

Orange signs backing up vehicles
Rotating lights stopping the quick handed
White rolling boxes saving souls
Long like limos, there the last ride a life goes

Under the weeping willow umbrella tree
Travelling under mountains through man made tubes
Below the urban surface, electric rails fly by
Foundation supports but can be cold

Candle with hot wax
Government dispensing much tax
Wireless messages sent through the fax
That plastic card is at max

Unheard voices
Yet to be seen places
Known sciences about certain insects
What reminds you of yourself best?

Monday, May 12, 2008

Pen Scratching

No matter your grass seed power
Dandelions will over tower
Ragweed causing millions to sneeze
Trying to score weed from trucks of yellow, just a tease

Fuel powered brooms dusting street surfaces
Electric sucker pulling hair from carpets
Fossils from the past are found in tar pits
Air from early sunrise chilling, wear hand mitts

Ants form a vertical line from window to door
Potato chip bags litter this floor
Back packing through a distance forest
Watching mystical mountains sore

Frozen doors on fifty cent telephone booths
Ones with more multi coloured bills use blue tooth
Strolling on slippery wet stones
Wondering if this water has seen eyes, completely unknown

Ship in distress, systems down
Morse code is sent for the SOS
People drank stubby Molson golden
Those moments blurry, the story changes as its told in

Trees standing shorter as deck space
Genetic foods developed with lack of taste
A sea of houses now floods an old country place
Stand against villains with sprays of mace

Everything lives cause of rays from a sun
Many female friends, call us male friends hun
Watching young lives cut up beef and not use the bun
Trouble comes forward many well run
Boulders falling from the sky little earth is done.

Wednesday, May 28, 2008.

Still a Chance

Swimming in a pool of water
Son of a mother
Every day she wonders
Who's the kids father

Never regretting the decision
To bring a new life
Within in a world
Of many possibilities

Twenty four hour time spans
Come by
With continuous routine
A new man in her life seems unseen

Every dawn starts early
Every evening ends late
Where one night at a party
Two teens got drunk and she got pregnant

He ran off
Most breed of man
Can act like a dog
Just like hair causing a drain clog

Mommy mommy
He cry's out
Not the voice of her son
But a father that ran, now begins to pout

A day might come
Where the male figure
Might return
So his son just doesn't have a mom.

Friday, May 31, 2008.

The Found

The word of others
Tends to be broken many instances
Trust can not be given to a strange mind
If you believe, could be mislead

Foundation under the water fountain
With old leaky pipes
Pressure weak and disposed
More fluid coming from a garden hose

Elephant sitting in sand
Tusks of ivory
Worth more to poachers then there lives
No more well creatures tolerate

Stranger walking the street
Afraid to see those eyes again
Fill with fear and discomfort
Avoid breaths in the tube tunnel

Liquor machine dropping bottles
Some enjoying the rush of taste
Some abusing the rush,
No care of taste

View finder has in range
Towering sculpture of the lands
Symbol for an urban garden
Rises for the second heavens

Lost in thought
Broken down minds
No matter a price
Some will sniff deadly lines

Voices from the distance
Area codes of costing
Undercover from rain
Reptile species bath in fresh water drops

Luxury rolling on rubber
From all points of direction
Vision of dreamt being
Down by a lake, this city is breathing
Toronto, Ontario

Saturday, June 15, 2008.

STANDING WITH A CROSS

Demons breathing fire hoops
Underworld for the damned
Cheating, lying, stealing
Well arrive you at this portal

Trying to make yourself feel like a saint
Taking lines a angel dust will not reverse your fate
According to ancient scrolls
Be good and do what you're told

Views of many in a vast world
Questions override few answers
Stay true to beliefs above water
Breaking the written, going to land you under waves of cold

Concrete stones mark those of deceased
Every wonder who's at the red gates
Or ones who are in total peace
Were only left to guess

After world of living maybe
Reading, currently existing
Live now, not later
Before you become a dead soul in a refrigerator

Thrive by the rules
Break everything look like the fool
Live by your stem of religion
Before floating to the surface

Sunday, July 6, 2008.

Stranger of the Dust

As the dust settles on the ground
People emerge from behind in surrounding vehicles
A golden circle tries to shed light
On a twisted metal scene

Two automobiles wedged onto one telephone pole
Clear road, no dangerous weather
How can anything slide out of control?
A chance for the ordinary to become heroes

Time for an ambulance to arrive
Has not been given as one vehicle burst into flames
A blue Dodge mini van slides into the ditch
Single man jumps from the driver's side

Not caring for his life
But only of an unknown other
A window explodes due to intense heat
This ables him to pull injured from the firestorm

Sound emergency vehicles are heard coming
He whispers into there ears
Relax only a few more minutes and they'll be here
Currently all have survived the wreckage

Paramedics rush up to the occurrence
Officers block access from moving traffic
Through all the chaos
One vehicle blows sky high, before the fire can be contained

A survivor asks where the man is
The man who saved us
No one knows what they're talking about
There is no one else here miss

Help of an invisible stranger
Has saved the life of five
An accident of total mayhem
No one will ever know who I am

Friday, July 11, 2008.

Depth of courage
Insight to imagination
Deflation flattens your tire
Appreciation fills your hopes

Your found in a city of many
Corn stock can not remain steady in high winds
Blood from her veins feeds children of the misquote
Mystic visions appear when baked

The friend I am
Is the friend to you
Take my hand
Experience a sound romance
Of friendship

Overpass fly's overhead in still movement
Diaper prevents flooding of nasty proportions
Cross walks protects the non polluters
Fire engine of red, tries to save the already dead

Kiss on the lips, truly angels paradise
Some wealthy step on us like dogs
Lying on a couch, staring at the tiled sky
Depending on ducks to eat white bread

Feeling on top of this world
No matter what we got
Or doing are best
Giving our true one shot

Window cleaner electrocuting your computer screen
Invisible flow of music vibrating window pains
Cleaner of the streets, be careful around homeless feet
Preserve value in ice

Rotating blades above, keep the floor below cold
Green coloured lantern causes streets to adjourn
Ears ringing from echo's of loud fun
Be careful where walking, don't trip over that string line

In the middle one last time
Standing here is not a crime
Friend this is my gift to you . . . .
ZigZag

Tuesday, September 2, 2008.

Chasing Unicorns

Look there is fog in the distance
Half a rolling hill in close view
Grass clean an crisp with morning dew
It's kind of cool in the air flow
But not cold enough for snow
A sliver of sunshine pierces
Through this thick fog cape
Perhaps soon the grey will lift off this landscape

The air dancing around gets warmer
Fog begins to dissolve
No longer being trapped in this corner
Sky is blue and doesn't stop the rain
The golden globe projects its beam
A rainbow spreads its hand
To where I look up an stand

I am looking for the elusive creature
Maybe you know its name
All white, majestic, powerful and strong
I would imagine somewhere it has its own song
Thought I saw, but maybe I didn't
Thought I heard, but maybe I couldn't
Thought I felt, but maybe I was dreaming
Thought you saw, but maybe you wouldn't

We're hear now on its turf
Some say its real as a smurf
Has to be real, nothing else has so much beauty
Maybe I'm on a buzz, impaired judgement
Crazy, insane, under the weather or in pain
No none of that, much the opposite
I am beaming like the rays on my face

LOOK! There it is in the distance
Its eyes are locked on mine
Even as it could be the last time
Slowly makes the journey towards me

Feeling nervous, feeling shaky
Kind of the butterfly effect many describe

Like love itself, it's all very mysterious
You think your getting close
Finally finding that connection
Feeling that one of kind flow
Like a bolt of lightning, it all lets go
The lights shut off
Thus ending this current I thought I was close love show

Elusive creature five feet from feel
Slipping on the wet grass as if it slipped on a banana peel
I blink, an this creature disappears
From my memory reel
Gone, no where to be seen
Vanishing like paper in the wind
Back to square one
Where this all begun
Feelings to describe my current mind
None.

Saturday, April 6, 2013.

DEATH VALLEY

Backed up on both sides
Bottle necking crammed highway bridge
Hundreds of feet from the rivers surface
The structure appears strong and true, but extremely weak

Six lanes of vehicles large and mini
Three kilometers stretching over the valley
Two years standing
One more second until its falling

Huge shutters shake the minds of motorists
Some think it could be trucks crossing supporting bars
Good theory, but no traffic is moving
Tall braces of the bridge appear to becoming down towards the roadway

Everyone starts panicking
Rear ending drivers in front of them
Breaking arms and legs
Screaming of the young and old

Brave ones not on the bridge see the occurring danger
Some dial for help
Others without even thinking run to aid threaten souls
Time ain't playing sides to who survives

Suspension cables break like sticks
Concrete cylinders crumble like crackers
Pavement rips apart
Middle disappearing from eye level

Running for there lives
Both bridge towers drop at once
With a sound louder then explosions
Cars being crushed into roadway

People dying without a doubt
Rescue helicopters nearing the scene of disaster
Hearts pounding, as more asphalt slips away
Water below filling with exploding fluids

Everything seems to slow down
Even becoming silent
Is that what happens when your soul tries to out run yourself
Each step towards land doesn't feel any closer

Don't turn your head to see the road almost vanishing beneath your feet
One huge jump in front
Cause of melting structure
Push off with both feet, five, four, three, two . . . . , one . . . .

Made it to the other side, alive
As the rest of bridge slips into the valley
Exposed electric wires showering sparks
Turn water to shooting flames

Highly doubt anyone survived the fall
Or at least praying that they didn't, to avoid the current pain
An emergence choppers engine gets choked out by thick black smoke
Crashes and falls into river of fire

To this day its not known how many fell
As a token of respect the vehicles and bridge remains were left at bottom
Represents where many lost there lives
Ones caught in danger
Others trying to save ones from danger

It was a year ago this happened
Here I find myself throwing flowers into the valley, for the fallen
Trip of these flowers
Shows the terror that all went through . . . .

Thursday, July 31, 2008.

Automotive Merry-go-round

Ford Escourt
Cadillac Escalade
Honda Civic
Chevrolet Malibu

Just a couple of makes and models to name a few
Driving in a circle
Larger then the base of Skydome
Girls of the night, bitches, straight and gay
In a way that Jordan always says HEEEEY

Round about, no
A place where strangers can socialize, yo
The road goes North and South
Center middle is the night club, Circle of No Doubt

From the sky headlights spin
Much like a children's Carousel
From the ground, windows are down
Beats from the club, keep the vehicles turning round and round

Meet your date on the spinning circle
Before you kiss under strobe lights in a one of kind club
Nabil using his line, how old is ya?
Stop an F-150 is the opposing lane
Introduced to twenty one year old named Elaine

If your wheels ain't rolling
Then your not with modern strolling
Girls on one side, boys on the other
Who really cares if he or she has a brother

Using one second lines
Majorly limiting your effective time
If the opposite vehicle stops
Your night might get very hot

Street lights pump there pink and blues
Shining the pimping colours down on you
Cruising at over fifty
Your ride looking mighty nifty

A girl finds you by twelve in A.M.
Well land your feet in the door
Later then this time
She may want a little more

An automotive sensation
Play games with all imaginations
Feel the movement asphalt
Believe us, its not your fault

Toyota Echo
Mazda Five
Nissan Altama
Funk Master flex may soon pimp your ride

Rotating like seconds on your clock
Tarmac rolls with rubber wheels
A new way a new feel
Maybe this girl will reveal

Traffic always flowing
So called pimps always rolling
Under fire from Government tolling
Knocking all ten pins down in bowling

A night soon to be finished
With the massive spinning circle
Record on the DJ table
Controls the rubber rolling flow

One more song of the night
Will you see her wearing something tight?
Till the end of the night you stay
How much gas did you just burn away?
For one night of play?

Friday, August 8, 2008 or (08/08/08)

44

One Story Apartment

The cd is broken   Stop talking clean the kitchen
Ford is out of oil   Hurry up care bares are on at four
Your cat just whizzed on my rug   Best cat ever
Plant needs water   Where's the DVD Harry potter
Guy at door needs help   Mental department is up the street
Turtle needs food   Keep your voice down, don't be rude
You're being rude   Time to turn up the volume
Pull the plug out from the TV   You're asking for it, pulling up the selves

Stop drop and roll   This living room needs a striper pole
This house is on fire   Don't make me call you a liar
Watering down with the hose   Have you been borrowing my clothes?
Why are you so dumb?   Why are you no fun?
I'm going out for a bit, see you later   Hey I just found my old pager

My roommate is the biggest loser   I've tried my hardest to get into that police cruiser
Just sits in that chair   Close that window I hate fresh air
Doesn't move around   Hey man, are still afraid of clowns?
No matter what I say   Just got another girl, time for a lay
That kid never listens   Your like my parents always bitching
Time for things to change   Does this duck hunt gun got good range?

No more crap Phil   I am just here to chill
Your turn to clean the apartment   Why? you're the one that pays the rent
Now I got a reason to kick you out   Come on Jean don't pout
Time for you here is done   Dam I'm scared watch me run
I will call the cops   I bet you will not
Not paying your way sir?   Phil you are a jerk
Pay now or leave   I have a hundred dollar bag of weed
No way its to late   This toke I will appreciate
Phil it feels like I am being used   Dam Jean that's old news
Welcome to my life living with you   I am sorry I was playing the fool
Thanks for admitting your mistake   Now let me cook you a steak.

Friday, September 26, 2008.

To, much water
To, much fire
Thanks to red hot magma
I have four flat tires
To, much feelings
To, much the same
Not enough criers
Not enough people to blame

To, much wood
To, much air
Trying to make it to the top
Ever right move seems unfair
To, much talking
To, much staring
Not enough saying
Not enough caring

Feeling right
Feeling good
Doing the right thing
As you always should

To, many insults
To, many bad quotes
Boat is sinking
Hard to keep afloat
To, much cloth
To, much paper
Not enough good ones
Not enough takers

To, much loving
To, much touching
To, much everything
To, much nothing
To, many fakers
To, many liars
Not enough real
Not enough buyers

Feeling right
Feeling good
Doing the right thing
As you always should

What? Huh?
Are you talking?
Can't hear you
I am shopping
What? huh?
How you say?
Tried my best
Can't help you anyway
What? huh?
What you mean?
You're feeling dumb
Like overcharged gasoline
Tire, huh? feeling good
Broken axle, what they say?
Maple tree, how you would?
Video phone, yes I know!

Feeling lost
Feeling cool
Feeling helpless
Feeling true
Feeling great
Feeling awesome
On top of the world
Like a new spring blossom

Feeling right
Feeling good
Doing the right thing
As you always should
Dream it
Live it
Don't give up

March, Monday 23, 2009

Open World

I grab your hand then your other
As they come in contact with me
I kiss your sweet tasting skin texture
Beauty for your face, needs to be redefined
Creation of those angel blue eyes
Must of taken extra points of time
Worlds most sweet flavored fruit
Cannot compare to
How much you look cute

Would I take care of you?
Whatever the moment I owe
My feelings will never slow
Let me kiss you bulls eye on those juicy lips
Let me hold you close
My hips line with your hips
Love stronger then any steel or rock
I'll put the card outside our door
So no stranger or known can disturb and knock

Global warming shouldn't be the fear
One of my main concerns
Preventing those magical eyes from sad tears
Stand against me, feel my heart beating
If you listen hard you'll hear my love
Trust me I am not into the field of cheating
Like a fantasy dream
Everything I feel and say comes true
It sticks to your soul like fog or steam

Talk of the million dollar wound
My always ongoing unconditional love
No matter the happiness or doom
Through sunshine, snow and rain
I'll do my all to protect yourself
Except if you find another and switch lanes
Everything is considered to most, the miracle
Going beyond the laid out box in the sand
Giving you my ring forever and my hand

The love from this one boy
More then any other that came before
These now and future memories, should be the cause for joy
Words to stand the test of time
Honestly, forever, truly, non stop, for real
These are the feelings of mine
I'll stand tall and strong with you my love
Go beyond as well as way above
For our wings to fly for eternity
The same as heavens bird, the dove.

Hands

Lost the words that I wanted to tell you
No matter the courage that back these bones
My love for you, will never be told for you
Being kept in my spot
Don't want your boyfriend to find out my caring thoughts

Carry on with your everyday existence
Don't worry about me
As you have no idea what you mean to me anyway
Keeping my mouth shut
Like a respectable gentlemen should

With a cross locked in my palms
Everyday I get on my knees and pray to god,
That you will be safe all moments of each day
All members of heaven as my witness
Deep down inside of me, I hope you always remain happy

Can destroy your current relationship
But with angels in my blood
I refuse to proceed in wrecking a perfect thing
So angels in me have agreed to protect you
Do to current situations I am not allowed too

Some days I'll be able to talk to you
When your granted time online
I will look forward to this technology enhanced conversation time
You'll never know these minutes are the happiest in my weekly occurrences
Tears falling from my eyes, will signal your laughter and smiles

I am the other man
Never had a chance to ask out your hand
As motion continues to move forward
Looks like my chance will never come up
From the first second I met you, I had already lost

Gained another really great friend
Definitely well respect that until my end
No matter what happens, it appears you will always love him
Hey look your smiling again
Must mean tears are soon to come from me

Didn't think I would say much this time my friend
After all, it was all me that actually did the talking this time
My feelings for a friend I can never revel, or I might lose her as a friend
In life you have to consider what's best for friends, keep their interest in mind
But at the same moment, a part of you will want to say I love you, and I want you.
Whatever you decide, **`Tears are Happiness,`** just remember that.

Wednesday, August 27, 2008.

Greasy cheese stuffed crust from Pizza Hub
That twelve inch grilled chicken sandwich from Mr. Sub
Fried over cooked lack of chicken from Kay F See
The McDicks trend, why do they sell over priced iced coffee

East Side Mario's with tons of free white bread
Laced in running butter, why can't I get black instead?
Kalc's for the lactose sensitive stomach redneck
Old man eating this strange food, wished he didn't forget his meds

Rugs making life die, I mean drugs
Roofs making minds wasted, I mean booze
Rigs getting you addicted, I mean cigs
Reads make plants that come to life, I mean seeds

Eh & W introduces the uncle burger
Burger Kink makes the skinny large, what a merger
Timmies welcomes the breakfast lunch
I'm thinking many calories, once again just a hunch

Montann's serving poop coloured soup
When it hit's the bowl, dark brown will be present, not to be rude
People eating shafts from a shop named after a train
If you drink enough of Wendee's water, you'll make it rain

Lace, oh snap I mean dice
Nintendo, dam I mean clean that window
Playstation, come on resist avoid the temptation
Wii, to much liquid I need to pee

Swiss Chalet the fries are yummy
Lifestyle condoms will make your mattress funny
Eating roasted cheese bread from Quiznos
You forgot the rubber, I guess you're the schmoe

Jackastors please draw on the table
Different coloured crayons for the slightly unstable
Not so good tasting plates from Bee Pee
I've just been bit by a mysterious creature

Junk food
Pasty jazz and crap
Coors light is never on tap
Watch for these strange places perhaps
Just follow this map

FOOD IN MAINSTREAM

October, Saturday 18, 2008.

Actually happening

High up in the stars

A family of four head to the Rocky Mountains
This day skiing on some of the higher peaks
All experienced enough to keep up
Even if snow chases and falls
Sun shining bright
No clouds are traceable in earth's sky
Snow sparkles away in children's eyes
Still this day is yet to hold much fear

Don't tell me they plan to ski down that mountain
I do believe they intend to my trainee
Has no one warned them of the threatening danger?
Not even one word of warning
Don't you think we should do something?
No answer, just terrific
Now my duty to watch over this family

The four members strap on there gear
Helicopter is heard starting up its engines
It takes a ride to the top
Father's son shakes the manager's hand
Assuming their safety is the companies plan
Lifting off the ground heading for the glazy peak
Tree's rising for the sky
Almost seem to weep

NO, NO, NO, don't leave that helicopter
You will not survive
Why does the living not listen to there inner soul
This snow pack is to become unstable
It will be way beyond your control

Skies kiss to fresh snow surface
Starting the descend towards the human ground
Everything going swell, sunshine on there backs
Fresh powder jumping up like loose dust
Son, daughter, mother and father
Feel like the kings of this world
Nothing can stop this good feeling of racing down the mountain

Maybe nothing is going to happen
They seem to be smiling and having a ball
Perhaps I am just being over cautious
This family well probably not fall

Earth underneath the snow
Begins to shake and break
White gold starts to run towards the ground
Family of four is soon to be found
No matter what they do, this wave can not be out ran

Flying down with heavens chopper
Trying to locate a snow covered family
Radar systems that are designed to find breathing bodies
Land on the site of the fallen

The Father

A man dug me out, wearing nothing but, shorts, sandals and tropical t-shirt. In the
distance I could hear the sound of a helicopter running. Was he a rescuer? I am
still fully unaware. But he kept repeating the same words in my ear, listen to my
voice while they dig you and your family out, hold on to my hand tightly, it won't
be to much longer. Once I was out of the snow, there appeared to be a steam shovel
digging more of the fallen snow pack away from the rest of my family. The air felt
warm like something felt down South, which didn't make any sense to me. The man
with the shorts on was directing the whole search and rescue operation, he knew
exactly where he was digging, and found my family. After finding them, he came
and sat down beside me and said "they will be here shortly, just hold on a little
longer". I said back to him, but were already safe, you saved us, he started walking
towards a helicopter. What's your name atleast sir, so I can thank you? He stopped
and turned around, I am the one who saved you, that's all he said, then flew away.

Sir, sir, are you alright?
You were just in an avalanche
The rescue teams are going to take your family to hospital

Job well done trainee
Why thank you sir
Just doing what were suppose to do
Being the miracle of life

You are all lucky to be alive this day
If it wasn't for this father's quick survival instincts, you all wouldn't be here
But wait the father goes
I didn't save them it was the fellow in a tropical outfit
What are talking about sir?
There was a man that was digging us all out of the snow

To this day the mysterious man was never seen again by the father, no tracks were found to suggest a steam shovel or helicopter. But what is a mystery to investigators is how the father digged his family out, including himself out of seven feet of compact snow.

I was saved by a man

UNSTILL SILENCE
Friday, September 5, 2008

More then Words

Feel the water from high peaks
Heaven's reality closer then death
An amazing place has a trait
Paradise where an all mighty might call home
Words can't describe it's feeling

Dreams come from here
Tears on her face belong here
Emerald blue eyes, created from its waters
Peaks covered in clean white snow
Frozen water falls are surrounding its scape

Night stars spend day light hours here
Trees of green stand in the shadows
Cultures of all sorts come to visit
Seeing nature at the finest state
Not realizing it belongs to a greater power

Streams cold dead to touch
Thin breathable current is what's up here
Warming of our mufflers is affecting its healthy state
Choking like a man dying from lung cancer
Future for a magic place, faces much trouble

Where we live we can't find justice
Money over sense of a future reality
Saving a heaven would be great
Apparently were going to take it down
As we would are own fate

Endangered species roam in forests
Cold flow keeps us from them
Or the golden fence of life
Sky's of gray invade this valley
No need to fear, its only rains from high above

Help me breath I won't make it
Stranger try's to revive them
Can't be helped no matter the effort
People aren't having troubles
Just the ice and snow cry's out

Winds will blow cool for now
As a winter sets in for some months
Past words point out, no matter what
One day this paradise will be forgotten
Tears now well only melt it away quicker . . . .

September, Saturday 27, 2008.

Sitting on a plastic aqua coloured chair
Directly in the middle of Memorial Avenue
A scene of despair is taking place behind me
Emergency vehicles of all sorts litter the pavements surface
What has happened just look past my left shoulder
A semi truck black in attire sits idol with its four ways blinking
One individual lays backside on the idle street
Looks like a no life left silent zone
His eyes our closed like this section of road itself

Is he alive you ask?
For this question, I fail to have an answer
Lets follow the ambulance when it heads to a near by hospital
Broken glass, a skateboard, shoes without feet, yet a sunny sky
Such beauty that surrounds this tragedy

Still sitting in this aqua coloured plastic chair
Beside the bed of the injured
Can't help but hear the other stories of sadness that surround me
A man in the bed across is coughing, sounds like a mighty suffering
His nurses tends to his distress at best, with some Advil
Wait they are going to move him to another location
Through the nurse an patient chatter, I discover he's 90 years young
A long lived life, I bet with a fair share of joy, but never to know where he goes

This individual from the scene barely breathing, not even 25
Can't help but wonder what life experiences he might not see
What people he might not meet, or the girlfriend he may seek
Harsh the circumstances has brought about here
I wonder why some go earlier then others?
Maybe its there purpose, a ripple effect might change certain laws
Expose our society flaws

Time ticking by oh so slowly, perhaps even backwards
Different seconds for every single one of us
These are not guaranteed or even earned
Just another element of life, like rain, sun, trees
Live them while you can, enjoy any moments granted
Cause at any moment of anywhere could result in a flat line
Try not to fear, nor worry, control isn't yours, so just let go

My aqua chair is gone, no longer sitting
But lying in this bed, I can see but not respond
A stranger sitting in a aqua chair along side me
Blurry vision in these eyes, I can not make out.
The clock on the wall goes tick, tick, tick, Beep._____
Sunday, May 27, 2012

DIFFERENT SECONDS

God dam new car smell on my breath
Sitting in a chair listening to Queen
Crazy Little thing called Love
In this seat getting no tug

Cat from across the street pissing on my mail box
Wondering why certain hunting seasons aren't allowed?
Can anyone find me somebody to love?
Highly doubt it, where's my camcorder?

My neighbor on the other side is really sick
And now apparently slipping away
Another one bites the dust
Earth's life keeps slipping day by day

Drinking driving in the end pay with your life
Smart jerk making the clearly stupid move
Oh lover boy
Where do you get your current love and joy?

The pre-season already claims of leafs losing
Clearly they are losing, if the branches are dropping them
Bicycle, bicycle, bicycle
Who stole my bike?

Fifth prong of this verse
Is it me or is the wording getting worse
Flash, savour of the Universe
Would you please stop my friends, some are jerks

Underground lost searching lives
Someone stole Phil's knives
We well, we well rock you
No doubt you already have, where's my stuff?

No matter what you punk's do
Losers no more well your pathetic souls are going to be
We are the Champions
Not stealing or other forms of thieving do we part take in

Steering wheels lased in leather
Engines full of high performance injection
I am in love with my car
Melting soon will be the tar

Hands clapping for my presence
Drums drilling my floor
Bass guitars breaking a clubs floor boards
But, fat bottom girls you make the world go round

View of a Queen

October, Monday 07, 2008.

The words floating in water
Speaking many thoughts to my ears
Predictions, no they are not
Past influences, yet again no be the answer

Sounds of a gentle flow
Transfer fragments of feeling to my bones
A language miss understood by many
It still remains as a real energy

Letters and sentences it cannot form
Pictures and slideshows, also won't be made
Images of dreams
Where only one symbol is recognized

No one individual can teach another this communication form
A mind must be born with this gift
Books on the subject don't and can't exist
As there is only mentioning's of this way

Found or lost
Living or gone
Started and born
We cause the fingers crossed, the holding on, and feelings of torn

The Stinging of the Bees

Thursday, October 16, 2008.

GRUEL SHARK

There are many happenings that take away
Away our money, soul and spirit
Like fighting the invisible battle
No matter how you act or claim
Certain people will take your life's gain

Saying help, help me
Will not stop the eating away of your inner self
Once material items have vanished
Feelings are on the chopping block next
Saying they love something, then days later denying these statements

One cannot stay strong forever with consist backstabbing
Being confused is that really an excuse?
Or a cover up for the greater truth
Some seven day segments go by
Words I love you, come back to the surface

Playing with my being
Becomes the puck in your personal hockey game
Coming to a point where no words you are truthful
Causing the fabric of space in my spirit
To die more and more every single day

Kisses of fiction
Heartless hand holding
Cold as steel snuggling
These were once warm signs of affection
Now finding myself cold inside and outside

Being more blindsided then a bat
Lending you funds so you can have food and fun
My bank account now broken
You laugh and smile thinking you've done nothing wrong
Me broke on the ground crying, my trust for you is now completely gone

Time to push away the tears
Needing the feeling to start fresh and walk down a new road
There's one thing you forgot
My heart you never really caught

Stay away from dark marquee waters
A creature waits to consume your natural resources
Don't let down your defenses
Once the Gruel Shark latch's on to you
Getting away, there are not many chances

Thursday, October 31, 2008
Inspired by true events

.

MARKED UNNAMED

Leaving the state of California
Only after a week of unsettled rest
Something is drawing me back to home
Your flight is set to leave is 15 minutes
I hope you enjoy your flight sir
Thank you, hopefully it goes by fast

Getting the earliest flight out of Los Angles
With a stop over just outside of Detroit
Didn't really bother my mind
Almost I'll be back where something is calling this name

Take off smooth no air disruption
Almost flying into heavens gates
A place where any king could call home
Concentrating hard seeing unicorns is not that far fetched

Hours only seem like minutes once touching down in Motor City
Stopover only one hour and thirty minutes of time
Overlooking Lake Michigan and the main freeway of this state
I'll sit down and wait

Twenty one minutes pass my watch
Looking to my left a plane can be seen coming in
But how come its coming from the East, when the runway is to the South?
Managing to quickly find an employee of the port
Pointing out to them the trouble coming down

Instead of climbing higher the jet sinks dangerously
Extremely low to the freeway
So much traffic it must be rush hour
Red lettering and baby blue cockpit races by where standing
Landing gear also not down

Left wing clips a free standing Interstate sign
Without thought crashing head on into fast moving traffic
Running with all speed, but still no chance to warn on comers
Eastbound flying into Westbound
Huge sparks are scene

Metal being torn away from airplane
Micromachine cars being vaporized
Tall true light polls snapping like thin twigs
Sound louder then any space launch
Orange bright terrifying chunk of fire rises

Running my fastest to get to the plane
Others follow my lead
Got to try and save
Fire spreading on leaking fuel
Every passing second creeping by, something blows
Another life is sold

Taking only five devastating minutes
Finally reach what remains of fire burning jet
Yelling at the of these lungs
ANYONE, ANYONE STILL HEAR ME
I can't hear anything but roaring of an orange lion

Finding a spot still untouched by flames
Squeeze my way in the craft
Seven young children are crying to me
Managing to get some help from another life saver
One by one we get the young out

Failing to find any parents or any other living
Start looking for survivors in broken cars
There's a women resting against a concrete highway divider
One wing of the plane is about to break over her
Going in without thinking about my life, only hers

Pick her up, saying your in safe hands now miss
Ground vibration strikes my foot
The noise of the wing breaking away
Thanks to the brave actions of another I am here today
I'll spare you from his happening of death
Now these are the words
The words that mark my tombstone and last breath

Friday, October 31, 2008
Inspired by a nightmare

Written text stories about smiles of winnings
Moving picture journey's of individuals with much success
Night dreaming fantasies that carry our greatest wishes
Where are the versions of people not making it?

Drowning on ecstasy fed streets
Harder, harder their heart beats
Liquor swarmed days
Believing that this pain will be taken away

    Imagine watching people always rising
    But somehow you never seem to be one of them
    This is a writing about a friend
    See where not winning may put you at end

Try, try, try again
A saying that parents of life
Repeat over and again many times
No matter how many times try, they never told you it was a lie

Same ones always become victorious
Don't seem to be room for us, little guy
Wrecked feelings from lack of fame
Everybody treats us, like everybody's same

    Notice the signs to prevent bad things
    A little word here and there, may bring back life
    Repeated non success takes a toll on one
    Smoothness in a road yet to come

Blurry on a street like the crushed tomato
Eyes staring hard on down
Face no smile only frown
Only thing keeping life going is royal crown

Summer plants soon to keel
A persons hands handcuffed to a steering wheel
Shooting deer to eat veal
Keeping words alive is the hard real

Rigged theft on judging contests
Trashed values to keep the better happy
Asking themselves an important question
Costs of losing the written art
Not keeping it together, but rather pushing it apart.

September, Tuesday 22, 2008.

Floating in circles in a yellow living room chair
Thinking many times to myself, that certain aspects of life are far from fair
Channeling through this sea of mistress, I find everyone I know
Taking part in life's dirty little secret
There beds floating beside my chair, watching not by choice many methods

By the written script of a devil, says I shouldn't even be visiting these waters
These waters belong to the cross the line kind
I'm not here in my natural being, only by bright light spirit
Much like a ghost haunting an old structure, there but not really
Maybe I just want to feel like the rest in this sea, do I want to pay the fee?

Long ago when the human body was being created, something was written
Not by our hands, but in the other forms that live above us and below our earth
Were all born as heavens warriors, but few make it to the end with that status
Our first few years of life, he with the horns leaves us all be
After about a decade or so, he will tempt you beyond reasoning

Seeing a luxury leisure liner sailing in the distance
Using a strengthened viewfinder I can spell it's name, Mistress
As the wind with the overhead night sky, whisper in my ear
With two oars and a vessel the size of a bath tub, I'll find my way over there
Almost as appearing to be slowing down, to welcome my spirits presence

Rowing up near to starboard side, its heart pounding
music can be heard by all close valleys
With sky jacked lights, brighter then any major league baseball stadium
Its tasteful appeal will attract anyone, who wants to have a good time
A rope ladder is tossed down to me, appearing to be polite staff inviting me on board
But well knowing that there hearts are as cold as the steel that the Mistress is built from

Seeing many friends I recognize, there's not much a warrior can do for them now
For the ones that took his sins, a tower where ones pry may help you out now
Alcohol and body dancing grinding are not the temptation,
it's the after party that sends up flags for alarm
Many on this boat have already have lost the battle, I'm
here to prevent anymore wrong doing
Having much to drink and dance to blend in, the horned king gives me power of his tail
To insert into the devils pit, of the female body

Jumping from the deck to just above the bridge, in a range of heavenly anger
I release his evil grip, now the crew aware of my true status I'll have to vacate

As not belonging to there cult, I in theory am not alive
But a lonely ghostly figure, that even scares the king of darkness
Like the flip of a light switch, I vanished into the seas

Even though the sea is large, an island of rather small square feet has the greater power
Any foreign vessel sailing towards our shore, will be sunken by the force of lightning
Lightning more powerful then any man made weapon of destruction
All us warriors are greatly out numbered, but the
technology in weapons far more advanced
Its said that the sun only shines on the dammed, and
night is for the heavenly, far from true

Going for a patrol, I sail by loose hands island
A sliver of land that belongs to all, and home to the dammed resort
Couples come here for pure hot romance, single virgins not permitted
Regardless of threatening signs, I stroll onto volcano grounds
A good friend somehow spots me out, tells me how her night is progressing

She assumes like the rest on the island, that I've progressed
Sorry to break it to you, any motives for me being are strictly non romantic
Warning her to leave immediately, cause of the approaching lightning storm
Also a number of warriors head for this site, for a mighty battle to claim this land
Instead of creating an army, the evil only created
temptation, making this its only one defense

Heavenly warriors have never had to fight using arms in a battle
Just their presence is enough to scare the skin on this devil
Loose hands island no longer belonged to no one,
It was renamed, Interquestion for the other side to think about motives
Forever its told, that the seas have no memory
But two islands do

To Progress further . . . .

Wednesday, November 12, 2008.

Frog

Your eyes are completely wide open shut
Wind dances around you like two lovers dancing at a ball
Rays of sun light rain down on you like droplets of water
Sounds of nature flow through your ears like fish in a stream
Light snow fall sticks on your shoulders like lost dandelion seeds

My eyes open and shine like high beams
Arms up high forming a V, from far away it looks like peace
Pearl white suit with pants cover my body's structure
Dress shoes covered in the colour black
Rock in middle of this glacier feed stream, supports only me

Sheets of many crammed with fact less knowledge
Computer screen melts into your head causing stress and pain
Thirty minute glass with red sand, a clock with no power drains yours
Electric blubs fail but birds still are able to fly
Piano playing in your brain, it never seems to sound the same

Feeling a friendly hand on your shoulder or wishing someone was here
Milk filling your cup, still one is missing making a hole empty
Pebbles in a shark tank, fade to grey when the creature leaves this place
Stiff freezing air with dark evil skies, cause much less good warm inside
Memories of the fun brings back a smile briefly, but disappear quickly like the winter sun

Dreams of your hands touch, bring warm nights
Remembering your sweet voice, when I failed to listen
Muffler on your vehicle rattled like a jackhammer, missing that sound
Nervous kisses from your lips, shaky but honest feelings of passion
Smiles on my face may never be easy again

Snow is glued to a mountain, like my eyes are still on you
Friendly non visible hands are from my souls own
Sleeps with the thoughts of kisses, are not fiction
Moments of remembering, are moments I'm still breathing
Still showing my passion from another point of life's cycle
Your night will contain sweet dreams

Wednesday, November 26, 2008.

How did I arrive here?
A sky that is half dark, half light
With shiny blue tinge
Cold arctic blowing air through my fingers
Shadow casting mountains behind where I currently stand

Far from any chance of life pushing forward here
Forests of trees and breaths of the wild would freeze
But somehow I only stand here in this blue sweater and jeans
Snow flakes crash over me like ocean waves
At first glance, appears what lands here never leaves

From up above it sounds like rotors spinning
Where I so stand, I cant make out any signs of image
White blinding snow blocks and hides view
A voice from behind, shouts out, is this you
No name of any kind is spoken, but just a word you

Someone is speaking for your heart
Emerson calls for it
Not knowing who that is, sounds like they are in trouble
Lit like a modern Christmas tree a chopper lands at my feet
A surrounding snow storm only gets worse in strength

Winds picking up much speed, sucking air from my lungs for power
Five minutes from leaving snow slick ground
Arrive overhead at a rescue scene
Life of Emerson has fallen through some thin ice, and might soon freeze
Swim I cannot, save this life according to someone's clock

Getting lower to where ocean tosses waves of ice
This chopper soon drops from this hellish sky
Into still solid ice, save Emerson is the dying's advice
Crawling towards an open hole in the water
I see the one holding on for their life

Just a few more inches, HOLD ON, I yell
Our hands are almost at touch
The breeze overhead is stronger then a brick wall
I'll be dammed if this makes us fall
Both our hand finally connect

Cold thick snow turns to hot dry sand
Waves from a Southern ocean are now behind
Once again alone, but now standing on a beach in warmth
A hand is placed on my shoulders, turning around to see
To see someone I clearly know, brings a tear to my eye

It is Emerson the one I saved from a cold water
Six Thirty, my clock rolls over to wake me from a slumber
A dream is all that has happened
But I still don't know anyone named Emerson, but the face I still know
You saved me mom, dream or not, I'd still save you.

Tuesday, December 23, 2008.

Pressured under the fluid trap
Hearing the liquid leaking into the nearby drain
Batch of miniature domes not meant for ones mouth
Instead expired wasted early
The trash cylinder breaths in there fumes

Its been awhile no matter what you think or say
Wheels are now again busted, better then sitting and rusted
Video in the camera was never broken, just frozen digital motion
Door lock releases, the old one shattered into pieces
Gears once again spin

Ingredient bowl jammed with ugly slimy colours
Drowning in a small lake of hot water and bubbles
Molded metal circle of many try to bath
Andy the cat runs when the liquid from counters top
Splashes the floor, making these tiles more trouble some

Leaning like Piza a bagged bin begins to descend
Overall pounds are to much for its weaken structure
A mess equaling to unfair dealt proportions
In a corner the raggedy mop even falls for the door
Trying to avoid its duty to clean up

Today disaster palace with a character called no luck
Tomorrow a new dawn to retry potential for the one luck
Super feet are the tires for the brain
Like nerves and gaskets they have been known to blow
Losses of creativity only for this day

Stick to your goal of desire, and one day soon you'll make your fire
Walls, bumps to prevent speed and fast balls will be heard
Success for the greater and not absurd
Role your dice
I do believe its your turn . . . .

Cheese Muffins

Tuesday, December 30, 2008.

He shouts wanting an object
For joyful pleasure which isn't in the gutter
Understanding a gift is what's needed from a giver
Two minutes can seem to last for much longer
This mind looking for the basics of happiness
Basics the average individual takes for granted
Sun shining blue sky days
Singing birds in a Maple tree
Little squirrels running freely through the yard
Boat horns on land, car horns from water
He likes orange original macaroni for lunch
Strawberry yogurt for the small snack
Milk flavoured cereal is a dinner time favourite
Keep your opinions to your most desired self
He won't take your insults
For someone to make fun, they'd be lower then a cockroach
Park slides, park swings, park friendly
people is a most desire
Snow tubing down a steep hill pure excitement
From six to eight at night is cartoon time
Flashes of lighting and the sound of
thunder, makes him ask questions
Rain droplets hitting the steel roof
give the feeling of peace
Friendly dog sleeps at the end of the bed
It's goodnight time for now
Soon a new day will arrive
Another day with Tinaca is the blessing
Because the doctors said, that he wouldn't survive

Monday, January 5, 2009.

76

Water Fountain

Sitting on a hard plastic chair
Hot standing still heat
Sweating skin like water fall
Fluid in this bottle
Long since evaporated
Fluid in this body
Has dried away
Every simple movement challenging
A few drops of liquid diamonds
Would make things much easier

Attempting to stand
For a far away
But short journey
Each step towards a destination
Seem to be intense extreme
Opening the wooden gate with knob
Could drain further ounces of might
Different air pressure tone
Greets this body
At the passage way

Ever so much closer to diamonds
Tiles beneath slowly float by
Gentle breeze comes from in front
Another birth arrived is heading for the destination
Legs can't move fast
Very little to nothing left
A show down race
Becoming of this
Like guns drawn in the West
Laces on these shoes come undone

Even if it comes to crawling
Knees down, palms down
Making mad last dash
Gripping handle of floating diamonds dispenser
But still looking head down
Pull up, pull up
Mind says to arm muscles
Like holding a runaway vehicle
Eyes, mouth level with spout
Cranking over odd shaped metal switch
Diamonds flow like angel eyes
Smooth steady and ready
Soaking dry sponge tongue
Battle for fountain, has only begun . . . .

Saturday, March 7, 2009.

Brief comments
Unreasonable jesters
False expectations
Broken promises
Everyday life
Same steps taken
Motions all but routine
Tripping over that line many times

Still have broken bones
Broken feelings from last injury
Swears made in stupid matter
Loud screaming noises in my drums
Morning, noon, afternoon all same
Eat your produce
Don't be late for the starting hour
No early minutes were left
With its phony blue sky
All mornings I see shower curtain butterfly

Meetings of none value
Gold fish could perform this task
Suggest fresh ideas of perfection
Once again fresh for rejection
Not one minute taken
Only for crushing paper
Trash can full of once hopes
Ladder coming out from under me
Don't ask questions
Keep sights low
Glass with rocks and rye
In the morning I'll see the shower curtain butterfly

Parts of many
Weather conditions are the only changes of scenery
Water cooler, paper cups
Coffee machine, Timmy's up the street
Retired vehicles, faded smiles
Hole patched, two minutes later hole scratched
Sweep dust, someone will fuss
Flavour gone, same old thing is wrong
Shower curtain butterfly singing its song

Ending of this
Fact heading for change
Furniture going to be rearranged
Blue sky
White clouds
Pink wings
Black eyes
Butterfly now moves along.

Tuesday, March 10, 2009.

Maybe wait for one moment second
Visions may appear at a stones throw
Feeling distant from others
As spectacular happening come before you

Give me space to breath
I've filled up to much on ecstasy
Losing my mind
This life is tripping through all space and time

Help me stay alive
I would prefer much so if I didn't die
Tonight well not prevent tragedy
Nor happiness and all sadness

Steady hand not your enemy tonight my friend
Drinking will not prevent disappear
Happenings occur no matter the reasoning
Maintain normal thought to get you through this spot

He's drank to much
Please, stand back as we try to reintroduce this soul
Brain waves clearly out of control
Ambulance pulling up to the side, well this keep him alive?

Touching a steal pole, reveals itself as cold
A ladder snaps in two, breaks and falls into the streets
Vehicle rolls over construction cone
As a car bursts into fire, well someone survive clearly unknown

Feeling pulled in friend
None of this is real, just a feeling of known, just incase these situations become real
Hold on for second, no questions this time?
Realizing the power of words, back off until the end, friend

Found in moments of thought
Dreamer of the future yet to be born, can they save us?
Throwing in the fishing line
Hours pass by, still nothing can be caught

Fallen on the ground I am
Please toss out your helping hand, my friend
Seconds turn into minutes, dying on cold pavement streets
No one knows friend, will I survive this feat?

PASSAGE UNDERGROUND

Friday, August 22, 2008.

We're running
Fast and steady for our lungs
The chaser feeling us out
Filling these brains with problem thoughts
Tossing legs forward to move
Obstacles keep leaping out towards
Trying to trip us down
Face first into dark green slop

This tunnel is coloured like night
But no stars shining down for fight
Electric beams fading in and out
Gainer is gaining its ground
Don't be stopping
Unless breathing is not important
Crazy, fast, pounding, hurry up, blood, furious
Our beliefs don't seem to exist

Bells overhead ringing strong
Something like fire giving chase
Time to take a breather
Not so far in this pursuit
Run, run, run
This tunnel has no mercy, nor end
Scary dreams have more grip
Water covered floor
Many more running seconds, I might slip

Feeling behind us halts behind
We halt in same matter
Catch some fresh puffs of air
Bright strings of light
Get brighter, them being the chaser
Steering head on into high beam
Expecting its motion to soon move forward again
Like the click of switch
Lantern tunnel turns dark

Silence quieter then death
Eerie goosebump shivers take over
Turning to look the other way
It's brightness returns
Flashing like a Halloween strobe light

Subway, train, truck
Have we lost luck?
Tossing our feet the other way
Like the wedding bouquet
Only friendly marriage doesn't greet us
Would rather get hit by a speeding bus
Running from fear once again

Fish swim in groups
People at a circus jump threw hoops
Help us, the hunt won't stop
Making a bold decision
Will either finish or continue life
Doors all around will not open
Must stand and confront
Looking into mirrors give this feeling
Eye to eye contact

Take this
Leave this
All around goes faded black
Left for unconscious attack
A friend grabs my shoulder
Drags me far back
Electric floating current, moulds shape
Wolf like in shadow
Teeth sharp like hooks
Eyes dark like great white shark

Tunnel of fear
Barking at us like potential food
We grasp each other
Hold hands, hold the wall
Engine and following cars
Come fast out of ghost walls
Train moves to still
Giving these minds chills

A once being
Emerges from phantom caboose
Lifts not moving wolf, from invisible tracks
This touch brings it's life back together
Without our stop

Haunted train
Wouldn't find the wolfs spot
A soul now returned and no longer lost
We all can cool down a little notch

Tuesday, March 17, 2009.

BROKEN FREEDOM

House in the overpopulated suburbs
Vehicles parked both ways on already crowded street
Children yelling louder then common sense
Basic same boring routine every single morning
Heavy flows of traffic no longer surprise

Think loud and fast
Is this your real dream?
Did you actually want this?
This broken down frustrating future
That you reject but try to except

Its Saturday welcome back to typical food purchasing
Another round of fuel from this same station
Complaining again your neighbour about property line
Child teacher meeting these kids keep doing the same wrong things
Pay check to pay check and over broke

Come on now
Are you really thinking about it?
Any insight is a good start
Is this really what you want?
Take a second, listen to your heart

Motion picture playing in over crowded theatre
Wishing the money was available to treat yourself
Driving under respected and powered car
Only vacation taken was alcohol induced imagination sketchy memory
Dive in head first into 1.5 feet of shallow kiddie pool

Is it taking grip?
The failure is freedom
What is needed to repair?
Repair what you actually wanted from life
What do you Really Want?

Rain leaking through that fresh nailed roof
Wallpaper and plaster crumbling to your floor
Grass overgrown and window cracked cause of thrown stone
This existence you're leading seems meaningless
A never ever ending going on forever eternity dragging show

Take steps needed for your true dream
Regardless a length of journey
Stick to your reward at the end
Remember that mostly
Cause it will lead
To What you Really Want!

KLEINGELD ES
(CHANGE IT)

Wednesday, June 17, 2009.

Shhh hear the silent membrane?
Voices traveling through air particles and moisture vapor
Fragment of mind is still like tree shadows
Grass blades are sharp like paper edges
Plastic lids float as if they were ducks
One second has finished, another begins the bid

Stiff like ice, watch out for wrong advice
Cardboard cup holder, addicted paper folder
Four zero seven electronic toll, undermined cereal bowl
Eight year broken bad luck mirror, yet the world seems so much clearer
Flight of a white fluffy dove, some say that's the sign of love
Speaker loud music playing, as age goes longer sound be a fading
Pryin to an almighty on your knees, to forgive your overcoming disease
Crowded line to the favourite ride, your heart pounding back and forth inside
Careful with those steps could get hurt, lose that concentration, have you met dirt?
An idea still thoughtful positive and strong, just
another single minute, please be strong

A photo picture takes form of remembrance
Last time intercuts of life struggle, not so fair
Clouds breath tons of CO_2 carbon
Looking out and over a shore line
Spectacle like none other about to come about
Witness the now born   Sunset Beneath the Stars

Sunday, July 12, 2009.

Shoe
Glue
Chew
Blow
Suck
In
Out
Sticky
Thick
Shit
Stuck
Expanding

Used as wood filler
Under the table when you enjoy a Miller
Sticking and stuck to your shoe
Some cases its used as strong adhesive glue
Patch the hole in dry wall
Good for measurement unless your tall
Spit it in the enemies hair
The explosion making everyone stare
Makes good for tire repair

Pink
Blue
Green
Red
Yellow
Orange
To many colours to compare

Multi ethnic yap scrambling
Over the hill cow yakking
Munch, tongue, rotate, bubble blowing
Yum, yum, seductive flavour punching

Balls
Big balls
Sticks
Squares
Rectangles
Blocks
Cylinders

Tubes
Odd messed up shapes
Looks means nothing, its all about taste

Delicious, tasty, yum, stacking
Strawberry
Blueberry
Banana
Apple
Orange
Cherry
Tastes from vanilla to tomato
That last mention better be a no

Double Trouble
Doddle Yoddle
Bubble, Double
Double Bubble
Bubble Bubble
Bubble Yum
Umm Bubble
B, Bu, Bub, Bubb, Bubbl, Bubble
<u>BUBBLE GUM</u>

Wednesday, July 15, 2009.

Kilometers and miles   Measurements for distance
Apples and tomatoes   Types of round fruit
Standing tall, sitting down   Do one or the other, don't fool around
Fuzzy dogs, fuzzy cats   You need a license for both of that
Rollercoaster, airplane   Can't stand heights? These will drive you insane
Bicycle, rollerblade   Helmets for both, where one or be unmade

Extremely difficult   Extra easy
Dress for achievements   Undress for the sleezy
Shorts, T-shirt for summer   Wear a coat in winter, it can get breezy
Ships a sinking   Sinking to on land with quicksand
Do what you choose and please   Ignore the giver of demand
Express your own style   Don't be the same as all other women and man

Going somewhere   Got nowhere to go
Stopped in line?   Over the line bouncing like a free spirit
Cd's and records   Both skip that favourite part
Books and movies   One keeps you awake, the other makes for sleep
Land and cell phones   Can't dial either without dial tone
Rubber tires, rubber condoms   Not having both will not get the girls of the
night home

Beautiful flower garden   Ugly, no need for elevated concert overpass
Clean light blue water   Polluted brown dirty water smelling like ass
Small tiny like an ant   Huge like an elephant, heavy with much mass
Quick instant email   Times have past for sending paper letters
As time moves along   Writing generally gets better
Turkey in the oven   Turkey alive has many colourful feathers

Hours and minutes   Measure the cruel nature of time
VHS and DVD   There's still nothing good on TV
Digital and analog   One is fast the other, not
Fast, slow   What you know?
Backward, forward   All positions of movement
Window and cardboard box   Both fill the gaps

Floppy disk, MP3   I still do know my ABC's
Wood or paper cut out   I'm still unsure what this is about
Outside to fly a kite   Still need training wheels on a motor bike
Need screws to mount   How many is six? Help me count
Asphalt or sand   Laying on both I'll still get a tan
Needing one more   Push button, fast forward
Were there   Are you prepared?

Sunday, July 18, 2009.

A Mad Television

Like the pond in chess
I stand before a black wall
Waiting for an unscripted land to appear
Where does mystery tend to take my imagination this round?
Light that was has all now faded dark
Start to hear faint noises of speech
Slowly dissolving in front is the black
Blue sky, light green grass, uneven elevation in far distance

Like marbles spilling out of a cup
I start rolling across the newly formed world
Seeing some familiar faces on the path ahead
Knowing them like a good friend
I hug them and shake their hands
Socialize as if were the trend were ending
Krista keeps looking my way
Giving me that cutie eye
Asking if it were wrong
Kegean, Micheal me and Krista are going to take a stroll
Birds singing all the known modern tunes
We talk up a sun storm of positive energy

A stronger breeze comes through park trees
Clouds tend to darken
I hold her against me for protection
That I probably really can't provide
Colour fades away like fire burning a picture
Were both on a boat
This vessel being slammed back and forth
In the roughest of bad seas
Rerunning an old movie
Scenery nothing but black and white
Holding on to the slippery wet water soaked rail
Not even a second for either of us to exhale

We both close are eyes
To avoid salt water sting
As we reopen the sun is shining once again
Colour has returned back to this less then unstable place
The vessel wedged between two dry rocks
People rollerblading around the decks like a rink

For purposes of fun making
Krista and I run around chasing each other
Having a time of our lives
She looks like an angel in golden sun light
Blue eyes, professional smile, perfect voice, lovely curly hair

Sit down on a bench to catch our breaths
Cuddle each other with structured arms
Like a instant slap in the face
The vessel vanishes out from under us
Both on our backs on wet sand
Sky is black with night and rain clouds
A major polluted city behind our heads
Freezing soaked and scared
No matter the messed up situation
We can never be prepared
Like a ghost fading into a wall
Krista is no longer in my arms
I am hear all alone
Walking the city streets of broken dreams
Doesn't ever seem that daylight hours live here

A hand lands hard on my shoulder
You're out of bounds, the voice speaks
No one second to explain myself
Dragged beneath a foundation
Brain now blackened out
Wake up with a device surrounding my neck
Not sure of the over all intent
One guy built like a battleship says to me
Find them, or you won't return
Find who?
Pushed out of a moving van
My lips kissing the pavement

Returning back to the beach
As I know there is no where to go
Sunshine yet again fills my eyes
A city washed away by the invisible current
I can see Krista again up ahead
Still wearing the neck device
All of a sudden breaks off like a piece of chocolate bar
Finding a random couch in a office with no walls

She sits down beside me
Holds my hand and kisses my lips
And says this world doesn't really exist
As I have been fighting its obstacles, I do believe does Krista

There is something moving around in the sky above
Crazy motions as it sways through the jet streams
Heading right for both of us
Blink of an eye
In a white single cab pick up truck
Driving through heavens country side
Small towns driven by farming the lands
Roads carve through like a hand flattening sand
Pull up to chip wagon
Or boxcar which it was
Eat some cheap food

As we finish up this meal
The sun is setting into its cozy nest
Krista kisses me on the lips and whispers
Please come back and visit another time
Tears come from my eyes
Smoke is starting to choke the boxcar
We got to save those people
They are alrighty safe, no one is in there
Out of nowhere all who I saw just appeared
Natural light and colours are becoming shakey and unstable
She says another goodbye
Fire alarm has gone off
Screaming like scared mind
Or is that a telephone . . . .

Saturday, July 25, 2009.
Based on a night time dream.

The Final Feather

Last moments of an individual's existence
Sometimes is said to be the precious moments in life
Whether they be a few hours, minutes or seconds
Regardless the fight to continue
A clock reading the seconds
Will always be ticking forward away

Strangers that do nothing but help them
Help them feel loved before eyes are shut
No matter the efforts presented
Its already been declared that they well be leaving
Tears heavy or strong
There story has been told
Time to bear the words, so long

Fog flooding the streets
Points of reference disappear from sight
Silence also sharing this place
Night time clouds always revisit this overhead spot
A day that at some points
Seems to be erased by all important standards

One second she said hi
Within minutes not by her willing
She had to whisper goodbye
Curious tried to save her through aid
When a life is already selected
Heaven says they fall through and fade

Natural and unnatural events claim
Like lotto machines
All is randomly chosen
No purpose for its decision
The rewind button doesn't work
There are no more chances for a second revision

A breath is taken, like a fire is set
Lighting or gasoline sparked its birth
Water is the ultimate one rejecter
Minute, minute
Hour, hour
Eventually we all will lose our
Light to power our flowers

Standing on a rock ledge
Watching a great lakes sunset
Sunshine sinks beneath the depths
A moon driven by current
Takes its place for awhile
Someone else watching
Might of been their last time to see a set

A friend will help
A stranger will surprise
A family will, sometimes it depends
A time frame will happen once
A life of anything will happen once
A flower will bloom once
A marriage will happen once
A feather will grow and fall out once
Another second will never be second, only once . . . .

Monday, August 3, 2009.

Florescent tubes flashing like amusement rides
School buses idling in a parking lot
People of deserving rewards are left in traffic lines
X marks the spot of what not to take
Snow is falling white, like angels from heavens earth

A brake I have taken
Fluid leaking all over the surface
It was a selfish act, leaving you
In the stand still function
Just remain calm as the mistake is repaired

Dolphins jump towards the sun, even if they can't make it
Having a dream, means you have a gift
Long cardboard nile, water leaking but still flows somewhere
Ocean front beach shows water and space for the wide open mind
If the sky isn't blue, that won't stop a person with a canoe

Rebuilding at a steady pace
After all that's what is needed to win a race
Games are long, were not all masterminds
Don't play a mind, please just enjoy their time
A joke can be funny, but don't take someone's money

Chapstick can only help chapped lips and not souls
Trees kneel down, not for respect but for service
A bug only bites skin, so it can live for another minute
Wearing the headphones of an MP3, still missing that golf tee
Saying never ever, makes you rather not so clever

Have you accepted my apology there friend
Maybe you haven't, I can respect that
After all I was never sorry
This is the glory of my long lasting story
Come back to town, for another round

Sunday, February 22, 2009

Moments before first waking for the day
Birds sing a good morning non rehearsed whistling
The trees wave their branches in the winds current
Almost as saying welcome to this day
Sunbeam lines up its rays to shine into my window
Spiders surrounding this property prepare for their daytime slumber
Bats get ready for a little shut wing

The pillow empty of another beside my head
Starts the morning same time tremor
A minor quake to say the least
These eyes rush open like fire hall doors
Yellow water fluid indicates a max capacity in the tank
A confusing few seconds as all mind and muscle power fires up the engines
First movements seem extremely painful, not the normal
Swallowing of air feels like, swallowing nails
Try to yell in fear, but vocal cords fail to function
Nose running like Niagara Falls
Flashes of heat seem to invade my skin and internal components
An unwelcome cold has pushed through my part time night defenses

Struggling to even breath, I creep to the laboratory
Bones creaking like worn out brakes on an automobile
Look in the fuzzy mirror, seeing an out of control brush fire as my hair
Can't even speak words of outrage, or words of any
Feeling broken, not even worth the energy to stand
Someone please put a booze bottle in my hand
Alone and laying on the bathroom floor
Wondering if normal life well one day come in store
Bracing my hands to the legs of the sink, I try to rise like the sun
Just like pushing a restart button, my engines try to re fire
Little to no success so far, now these ears hurt

Pass out thanks to no energy or lack of
Two more sections a sixty specs tick on by
Wake up to the day yet again
In same annoying painful matter
But attaining some new power to raise myself to sink level
Grab the canister marked a devil, pop two tablets
Wait for the pain to go briefly away
Time to find out if a man made indoor water fall can make this mess feel better
Hot, cold cranked over at the same time, same motion
These droplets feel so good against infected flesh

Music playing in the background, from the bee room stereo
Trying to sing even though I can't hear the words coming from my own mouth
But still at least dancing and feeling good
Its the attitude you bring to the table
Feel either great or let the unrest leave you feeling **Broken**

Tuesday, August 25, 2009.

People would rather see me
On the side of the road poor broke and die
Appose to that alternative
Spread my wings and fly
Everyone all around me
Watch several of same television shows
All there interests being no different
From ones to the next

A television in my corner
Rarely breaths light
Collects dust, rather then my lazy sight
Can't stand what the others all like
Help me fly like a bird and achieve flight
I want to go high and way above the clouds
With what we call life
Finding any followers with vision
Seems to be the impossible division

Don't want to be average
Stay at home with the kids
And bake the midnight cabbage
Where can I sit?
Where no negative seekers come
Stay away if you mean to create hate
Alone in this space
How do I change this image?
What are the rules to recreate?

It's if everyone wants to be in the shadows
Way below, down and out
Not at the top of the tree with misquotes an bees
At the top of a mountain yell, shout
Lose your grip, please let me go
Try and find the makers of my future talent show
A place where smiles are white
People are pleasant about all moments
Financial freedom rains king
No problems of any to worry over again

Join me father as we kneel and pray
For our work and efforts
And future celebrated day
Intense rotation being tossed all about
Dropped in the fountain like cheap change
Scrap my skin on a sidewalk
Watch it all be rearranged
Losing my patients with everything
Including this screwed up life

Calming down, realizing a reality
That one day our time well come
Not death, but a world of broken promises
Empty suggestions, no sense questions
Every day rejections, false intentions
One day they well all apologize
Remembering the trend setters
That wanted another path
With this certain success

Others well see the complete ROTATION

Thursday, September 23, 2010.

Venturing like lost animals in the woods
Compasses spinning confused backwards control
Electronic devices are flat lined, non responsive
Dead over weight gloomy clouds float around us
Shadows of ghost trees surround our lives three
Sounds of the flying cannot be heard
This place is as almost it didn't live
Air currents are far from warm, nor cold
Coming up to an clearing in the distance
Appearing as flat field with some sort of crop growing
Wooden fence protecting all four sides of this square
Looking for munches of treat, water for relief
A rusty sign unreadable to our sight
Maybe a caution warning of fright
Positioning our feet to overcome
This five foot lumber hoop
A shake in the ground below knocks us three down
Field sunshine falls shattering like glass in florescent light

Rusty gate hinge
Flashes, green, blue, black
Falling off a high ledge
Fuzzy jumping pig crossing screwed vision
Brown cat with pink eyes
Clothing hanging to dry and bleeding
Broken glass imbedded in skin
Flashes, red, purple, dark blue jack
Moose horns tossing this body
Panic freefall purple skin
Brain raging out of control with pound heart
Red lights do all and can't stop
Blue berry plants squeezing necks
Flashes, white, yellow, lime green
Birds flying still in strong winds
Stack of paper falling, emerging as a tree
Elephants stepping on mice, eating rice
Grass grows red, thick, damp
Tombstones melt ice into mud
Handcuffs holding down these limbs
Eye's rotating like beach balls on water
Flashes of colored light, strobe faster with each passing second
Help, Help, HELP . . . .

Rain dropping on these three faces
Covered in blue blood from the berry's
Dazed beyond reality
Puzzled like a death mind
Wondering what has happened in the last hours of time
Where did that field end up?

Stuck to the soil like glue
Struggling to stand up right
Overcast sky's dry up like desert sands
A blueberry with eight legs pops out of our hands
Sharp skin piercing web penetrates
Around they go, wrapping us in sticky string
Not able to move
In a standing prison
BOOM, BOOM, BOOM
Three extremely bright blinding strobes
With ground shattering thunder

Solid earth splitting like toothpicks
Falling without parachutes
Heading faces first into dirt fast approaching
Everything goes black
Eyes open to black automobile driven tarmac
A passer by calls authorities
And waits with us until they arrive
License plate on there vehicle reads, B1U3B377Y
Bumper sticker reads, The meadow
I look into his eyes
Flashes, green, blue, black, red, purple, blue jack, white, yellow, green lime
Every second always changing colour
His skin dyed blue, and hair like vines
Grabs us three, you'll forever be stuck in
BLUEBERRY MEADOW
_B1U3B377Y M34D0W_

Sunday October 4 2009.

Ever taken a look at your surroundings?
But not just a look, an in-depth analysis
A cloudy rain soaked morning, is a cause for joy
Leafs colored changed laying about our ground
Slippery no traction with modern walking shoes
Grit given on our feet, avoiding that slippery problem

Plant life breaths the same air along side us
Lighting littering this atmosphere gives them their green radiance
Echoing thunder quakes dirt to force up the underground
Now above providing a feast for those that swoosh through open skies
Water beads off tomato skin similar to water beading on a waxed windshield
Liquid bleeds through spider web, drip, drip same with leaky eaves trough

Rotting tree branches fill with small eyed insects
Until the roofs cave in they'll call this home
Surface appearances look like heavens garden
Facing underneath the view is much different

Fur on a creature's skin, acts as protector, fluffy blanket
Feathers decorate bird's structure
With breath taking shades of all delight
Beaks giving them there voice to speak and survive
Wings stretching from our moon to the sun
Floating atop us like forgotten angels

Wind breezes stronger each moment, erasing our summer paradise
Laying tracks for the inbound coming white snow season
A northern landscape changing, going with the times
Trees taking off their leaf hats
Grass surrendering its rich green texture, for worn down brown

The wild going after final food sources to live indoors
Cabin fever they may develop, a return to fresh air they'll crave
Fresh water pits well soon crystallize into frozen rocks
A way of freezing time, slowing down a cycle's process
Wave goodbye to the hot climate we forgot to have

Rein of Life

Wednesday, October 7, 2009.

My name is cocaine
My name is insane
My name is my brain
My name is a pain
My name is flashy
My name is catchy
My name is painless
My name is harmless

My name will leave you thinking
My name will leave you drinking
My name is fishy
My name is bitchy
My name is the bomb
My name is to long
My name can't get along
My name smokes the bong

My name is the speaker
My name is the bleachers
My name is the seekers
My name is the achievers
My name is a hose
My name is warmer clothes
My name is bigger toes
My name is not Joes

My name may seem loopy
My name may seem droopy
My name is applause
My name is a flower vase
My name is so damn cool
My name went to school
My name is not a tool
My name is your fool

My name is a knob
My name is a cushy job
My name is the bar
My name is fresh hot tar

My name is supreme
My name takes gasoline
My name is the dream
My name is on the team

My name is not a loser
My name is a juicer
My name is a cow
My name is so wow
My name is TV
My name is MP3
My name is so seriously
My name obviously

My name is so pretty
My name is so gity
My name is on that kitty
My name is what a pity
My name is CD Rom
My name is sex with no lights on
My name is made of glass
My name is worth a lot of cash

My name has been seen
My name on computer screen
My name is the shit
My name is on a mitt
My name on a pin
My name cannot swim
My name is a plug
My name means a hug

My name to many times
My name before 12:09
My name come on end
My name settle down friend
My name playing with scissors
My name has no sisters
My name hates winter
My name has a splinter

My name snakes and trees
My name misquotes and bees
My name pigs and frogs
My name horses and hogs
My name cats and dogs
My name swaps and bogs
My name slammers and pogs
My name walkers and jogs

My name is floppy disk
My name doesn't exist
My name likes to frisk
My name is so brisk
My name is a boat
My name will stay afloat
My name well here it goes
My name is R. S. Apple yo's.

<u>My Name</u>

Thursday, October 15, 2009.

Tripping over a sheep while trying to hop the fence
Dropping your pencil because you lack grip
Floor is all wet apparently somebody forgot to lay down a towel
Dialling the right number, while dialling the wrong number
Opinion of thought, blocks concentration
Engine idling with nobody at the wheel
Nervous hands, dried out fresh dead plants

Fish in toilet far away from tank with no food
Overflowing pool, wasting the clear blue fool
Ignorance forgot the sign, might as well smile at coloured pants
Reminder of flickering, save, save, you lost your work
Gloating up high with ceiling tiles, all are jealous because they are still fat
Frozen ice leaking pipes, damage expensive, your ego down the drain

All who use the P word are liars
Nobody with common sense has achieved this status
Somebody that claims they have, maybe they seek attention
Starving for eyes to look at them
Looking deep in their lives, watching them undress the belonging spirit
Hungry lions challenging the pry
Pry rarely care, no matter the competitor, we are here to stay

Trying to remember what was wastefully forgotten
Written by your own hand message, the item in question left behind
Uneven ground, legs stumble and fall, drunk sober walking
Special evening planned for many moons, now alone facing avenue goon
Melting pots shrinking in size, orange rings of element take the gold
Invisible talent thrown down the sink, made up memories visualizing failure

Another second for a clock to stroke, time is the tempory friend
Saying words of promise one instant, not one of your word
Behind the neighbours bushes laughing at others, their eye is on you from undercover
Dancing like an owner of earth, perception acting as all actions are smooth
Tasteless, tasteful delights available from all areas of breath
Put my leg out, trip you over the forward bar stool

Can't blame the one that played the prank
Paying attention to all surrounds you lack serious vision
By even saying the P in every way, shows the lack of P

Dragging those around you down, cause these loving eyes to look away
Get a sense of reality for one second friend
Your lack of direction, shows your lack of perfection
P- for Perfect, nobody.

Lying Perfect

Wednesday, December 9, 2009.

White, white lines flashing by the eyes
Your speed says how fast they go on by
Signs speaking of what lies before us
Other travellers pass on the side
Apparently they seek death earlier then the rest
Let them have their thrills before I
When I arrive, these places I well absorb slowly

Passing still much slower drivers then us
Perhaps they fear the future that awaits them
Not willing to step out of the normal box
Yelling as we pass, EMBRACE YOUR FEAR
A little motivation is all that's required sometimes
Destination is approaching ever closer
Each second more anguishing then the last

The sky out and dark
Never alone when improving you're broken down life
Street soaker reads a licence in front of I
Blink, blink lanterns flash along the shoulder
Nearing the point of don't return
Keep it short, keep it simple
Rings through these brains almost all moments
Maintain a positive beat, always repeat

Feel it, bumps in the road remove those butterflies
Traffic slowing all around
Blockage in a systems pipes
Prevent the flow from succeeding with ease
Remember that long term goal
This drain well be unplugged soon
Then run with your flags of pride again

Almost, almost at the finish line
We're moving once more
Making good steady streaming time
Boom, boom stereo pumping the great feeling jams
The mountain that stands tall in front
Will be the tough battle
Battles are won when everyone sticks together
A common interest, trying to be attained
Up in the distance, a black curtain sky is brighter
Nearing our achievement

I have to stop at this marker
Assist the stranded along the side
Being this is what we do
Helping the seekers returning to the road
With high positive full steam
I stand as one
But stand with many in rpm team

HIGH WAY

Wednesday, December 16, 2009.

Strumming a guitar beside a midnight fire
Individuals not necessarily singing, but relaxing to the rhythm
A soothing sound like this one being herd, warm these souls
Few claiming that even stars high above are slow dancing

Sailing towards a Pacific wonder
Glassy liquid surface acts like mirror to reflect a large sky
Monuments of land mass are lost from every direction of blue
Ball of fire over head, is the only friend on this shoulder

Flying over flat lands of Saskatchewan
Tractors plowing through miles of earth
Planting season soon to take off
Fresh product will shortly feed a Nation of thirty million

Openly now I'm on the opposite side of the table
Friend I am not sure how I got here
Simple thought comes to mind, someone stole my seat
No, I'm not accusing you, I just got here to late

Broken bones from critical injury
Needing the power time to heal these wounds
Being there at the wrong time costs money, also other loses
Rewinding time, if only that was an option

Since I got here apparently late
I've been told not to say much, just to let you enjoy the reading
Lets be honest I haven't said anything useful yet, so its your turn
Your turn to finish reading, without me, use your imagination to figure this one out friend

Scooping out a hole for a new foundation
Forever changing a landscape of peace
Soon to become a loud polluting landing of modern life
Future moves ahead no matter what lays before it

Were all given a purpose, so it is thought to be written
The prewritten is made to be changed, what do you see your self doing?
Travel get out there, follow the lines of the street, see where the landing is
Live life, do people, breath air, god dammit shut those curtains so people don't stare

Naturally I can't sit and not say anything
Still not going to say anything to constructive
Yes friend I am being a dick, but hey that's life
Just remember one thing for me, do your best at **Spelling Words**

Sunday, August 24, 2008.

The Umbrella Factor

Generation after generation pass down
Down the details of prophecies and tales
Warning of superstition at every single door and corner
Basically telling us to stay indoors
Stay under the roof of safety, still no guarantee of its protection
Don't breath in air, keep your eyes shut
Monster in the closet jumps out invading your safety zone

Mirror breaks shattering into millions of splinters
Pat yourself on the back, 8 years no luck
Open an umbrella indoors, click, poof, outwards
Stand back no rewards given for that harmless act
Watch the deep far down, miniature sidewalk crack
That can be claimed as attempted battery
Keep the link moving forward from the word of a stranger
Breaking the chain can cause anything irrational
Six, six, six dooms day random selection of same number
Should of avoided the temptation of opening an umbrella inside
The digit is thirteen, the day be Friday
Duck underneath your desk be prepared for the not interested

Dodge made up tales
Open an eye or even both, look for life
Don't be pressured from negative wanting you to fail non believers
Live as you desire, get away from the mass fire
Go ahead do the unsuspected and let all reject it
Lucky seven claims victory
Good news, great day, can't wait another minute
Smile on that face will push the overcast clouds away
Umbrella inside, you're welcome to have it your way.

Thursday, January 14, 2010.

The bell swinging back and forth
This old engine is getting ready to move forward
Steam flooding, consuming the platform
Passengers wave so long to their loved ones
Tears dripping down their faces
Rain droplets spraying all around
Wheels grip the track and pick up momentum

A stone lying beside the left track
Is sent flying up into the air
After all cars go flashing by
So far up it registers at 30 thousand feet
Ping right off a 747 reinforced windshield
Black and blue in colour
It screams across earths sky
Traveling to the forgotten location
Excited faces cheer as they near a warmer climate
That little stone gets stuck on the aircraft tale
Seeing a world beyond anything's imagination
Clouds inhabit this region
Perhaps angels with trumpets roam in these fields
Watching a civilization trying to get along

Veering hard to the left
Beginning its slow descend to warmth
The little stone falls
Racing towards a large ocean
Ping, bouncing off a vessels roof
Landing a top of a diesel smoke stack
This ship bound for somewhere with many material products
Crystal diamond blue liquid surrounds floating steel
Wind currents breezing ever so slightly from the East
Precipitation is closing in though from the South
No Matter all the effort
Out running this monster won't be achieved
Rough times are coming about

Ice starts pelting the windows, decks and ocean
Watch as the sunshine slowly dies away
Uncontrollable current drives this vessel into an awaiting shoal
Little stone bounces of stack
Splash right into rough salt water
Descending to a deep floor

Ping the stone clips a submarine
Wedging onto a rivet
Sea life dodging this man made missile
Look at the weeds as they dance
Fish swimming in groups
Twirling around like revolving signs
Silver, gold and sparkly skin
Sub keeps speeding off into the liquid darkness
Where is this mission going?

Light starts to become more apparent
Rising to the surface
Like the sun raising out of the ground
Cutting through surface water
Similar to knife and butter
Cold snow floats all over
Air freezing to skin
Boom a large shutter
Little stone goes flying off
As submarine ploughs into ice berg
Exploding fire storm engulfs all surrounding surface
The stone lands in snow

Looks like the final resting spot
Nowhere to go from here
Minus fifty degrees frozen landscape
Nothing can survive for long out here
As the flurries continue to fall
They bury the stone for all of forever
Until ping the ice melts from under it

Memories are what you want to remember
One day you will meet again
Just not right away
Enjoy the time that's made available to you
Don't wish it all to fade
The sun is melting fresh snow into water
Little stone starts to move again
A journey has only started.

A Stones Throw

January, Sunday 24, 2010.

Waiting to see vision in your eyes, stop with the lies, cries, every moment someone dies

Don't sleep on crowded shoulders, stay clear of jagged boulders

Intense stream out of control, have long term guidance, don't ever let go

Moments are aging with much anticipated desire, you hold the key or match to light a fire

Freedom steps to walk across an invisible pond, super strength adhesive molds our bond

Clap, clap, clap those hands, stand jump for joy while watching this band

Where were going is nowhere we've been, leaving the
known, gone exploring forget the sinned

Desperate acts call for disparate pleasures, follow the
already drawn map it leads to your treasures

Blessed tears fall from shattered eyes, avoid the consolation, breath underwater feel alive

Shamble, ramble, your breaking up, broken voices sing
uncoordinated rhythm, hurry up change the channel

Creeping upon you like a ghost floating through night,
don't run from fear, stand the ground, fight

Smiles sneezing loose and overly twisted, a final caboose drives by, you missed it

Maintain your thought positive, wishing star spawns the whisper of thee magical dove

Reframe from methods of failure, anyone simple quits, thus they serve a leader as a trailer

This minute is just another segment in time, be buried only
worth a dime, or go out there and attain your fine.

Monday, March 8, 2010.

Can't sleep a wink
Pulsing images of a close future
That I want to deny at this time
To SOON, yelling to a mirror
In no more then the one second dream
My brain must be broken, stuck on repeat
Like a broken record saying a same verse over and over
Panic, cold sweat, tears dripping when I awake

Late upsetting day
Before this unsettled night
Only hours of five are available for slumber
Eyes can barley stay open
No matter this obstacle, I still cannot sleep
No bodies to squeeze
Where are the ropes to hold?
HELP!! Yelling to mysterious colours
As my wall swirls like currents of water

A howling towards an overcast moon
Brings me out of devil breathing sleep
Five minutes before the set alarm
Even though I have awoken
Still sweating cold in hot water shower
Worrying is considered useless
How about overwhelming panic stricken bones?
I can't control these fearing thoughts
I think I am going mad even insane
No one around to share these unstable emotions
All alone in this dark universe

Sun rising from its lucky lazy slumber
Suppossive rays that spread happiness
All I can feel and see are impulses of craziness
Calm down, calm down
I whisper to myself
Music with its powerful beat
Usually settle me down
Nothing is working, everything won't retreat

Where heaven meets heaven
Feels like I'm at the portal for hell
Speakers saying there words of glory

Watch them talking, but hearing seems to be impaired
Invisible bubble of darkness surrounding me
All angles of attack on me are being taken
NO MORE yelling to myself
Make it stop, make it stop
Someone please hear my silent screams for help
Passing out from to much stress and unhealthy thinking

Out for many hours then the norm
A storm of insane thoughts and panic
Has disappeared
I feel normal again
Can't explain the method or anything behind it
All I know and want
Is no more ***Deep Impulse***

Tuesday, March 30, 2010.

Riding down a slide
On an not sturdy wagon
Shaking violently, yet staying perfectly straight
In hand miles per hour speedometer
Reading between 140 to 190
Turning into a spinning vortex
The slide extends outwards
Similar to a slinky stretching
Colours purple, white
Wagon maintaining wacked speed down peppermint lane

Vortex starts to dip randomly, speeds increase
From behind two friends of mine emerge
With similar radio flyers
Gravity clearly doesn't thrive here
A glow of light shines in the distance
Bending hard left, with nothing to grasp
I fly from the wagon
It rides, up side wall
Vaporises from view

Now in a space with black walls
Nothing with reference I can identify
Falling through an uncharted realm
I yell aloud
But no playback echo
No wind to great my body as I drop to nowhere
An end I pray for
Hard to pray when no one or anything to hear it

Something grabs my right shoulder
Invisible in appearance
Pulls me through a never ending fall wall
My body laid out on a baggage carousel
At a deserted airport
Those two same friends from that vortex
Arrive out of imagination again
Laura, Carley, how do you do?
Saying little to nothing they lead me to more unknown
Fires burning out of control in surrounding city
Yet feels like many dead still watching
Walking the lanes at a hospital
Some survivors have beaten odds

A middle aged man is running
From the other end of the hall
Wheedling a knife
Headed right for me
Hand gun on floor, below my feet
Without thought pick up the weapon and fire
Doesn't even effect his rhythm
Three more times trigger is pulled back
Still isn't slowing him down
He is not even saying words
Just drooling and making noises like an infant
One round left, aimed at the head
Sparks fly out the gun, target matched
Only described as a miracle

Sweating like a solider in combat
Trembling as if I were drowning in a shipping disaster
Now something can hopefully hear my prayers
End, end, end, END
Landscape fades away, and restores into a city
Before broken memories
Blue sky, green trees, birds and bees
The man I shoot at before the disease
I see, looking at each other
With a stranger wrong neighbourhood impression
He pulls out the hand gun I had used on him
In the future time

According to the track called time
My life must end here
So I can call with my revenge later
Barrel aimed for my skull
Purple and white peppermint
No wrapper pops out of my hand
Gateway to vortex perhaps?
I whip it at this mans face
Pin pointed directly into his right eye
Taking his goal
Vortex reverses the outcome
And spears my soul
A future changed
Now anything can be avoided and told.

Friday, May 14, 2010.

The worlds on fire
Flaming debris crashing all around me
Personal realm of mine is running out of time
I feel massive pressure at every given direction
The fuzz causing mass frustration
In my station of no nation

Looking up towards the heavens
Giant boulders free fall near my location
An old farm house in close distance, I race towards
Any given moment this night, I might lose my light
Invisible devil of wind is sweeping the earth beneath my feet
Trees, rocks, mulch and sod, suffocate my skin
No warning semi truck of yellow, levels the house
I'm standing waiting for the end, nowhere to go

Thee friends, have descended
Thee thoughts, have pretended
Thee olive branch, no longer extended
My life feels near finished
Why ask the words of the dim witted
This month has been hell; I can't take it another minute
A life preserver I do not seek
But a little promise would be more sleek

Complainers do nothing but complain
They only bitch, they never go for change
Love is it a destiny or a child fantasy
I see friends getting married and starting families
Mean while nobody anywhere well go on a date with me
Losing my grip on that positive train
Feels like my life is sinking in a drain

How can I pray if I don't belong?
I try to drown the negative with happy songs
Alone, non existent like a ghost
Like the last piece of bread, becoming a lonely toast
Tin can in the gutter
No other clubs just a putter
You're wrong its margarine not butter
Stuck on the highway watching your engine sputter
I don't want things to end here, a change just give me another

Checkmate as they say in chess
All I want is that ultimate success
Perhaps I need to vanish under the clouds
Maybe for a year or so, until I come about
Whatever it is I need to do
One day I shall emerge as what I want
Don't stare, hate or taunt
I will make it and become what I want.

Tuesday, June 14, 2011.

Look there is no one smiling beside me
No hand that joins mine and tells all will be fine
I dream big, while most others dream small
I feel lost every which way I go
Waking up in the mornings, sometimes I wish not at all
Somewhat depressing yes, so far I'm not having much luck on this quest

Rejection from all forms aim there way at my face
Some days I can't bare another moment in this place
No one seems to value my opinion
Negative comes from mouths of the masses
Everyone brown nosing, kissing asses

Help me to find the means of remaining here
At this moment maybe someone well be listening
Or the silence will prevail
The expiration date has come, an I already feel stale
People say I support the image of being happy
It's so beyond the truth, it could make you sappy

Like dark tinted glass on a car
Impossible to see what's really inside
I want to find that big rock, crawl under and hide
Can you hear my call for help?
Like a phone off the hook, it still goes unnoticed

Who wouldn't want to say all is fine?
News for you, my life isn't Disney
Currently this life is more then unsettled
Medical, work an other forms of stress
Affect me in all shapes, preventing me from doing my best
Still here for now
This isn't the final curtain bow.

Tinted Windows

Friday, March 9, 2012.

Writing on a scrap piece of paper
Because I cant find a normal sheet
I am feeling a little bitter
My computer and internet seem to be heading for the shitter
This room lonely and dark
The lamp over me blown, lost its spark
All I got for light is a glowing coca cola pen
T'was a gift that came from Atlanta, from a friend
No girlfriend in sight
This single business is really starting to bite
Losing some decent weight
Ready for some summer sun to create a tan
To keep losing the pounds, maybe I should eat Raisin Bran

It snows where I live
The dream to be where the earth is warm
Is one of the few that wakes me in thee morn
So hear my words, let me be on my way
To a life with functional equipment, a lady, 24-7 sunny days
That's where I want to stay.

THE DEAL

February 29, Wednesday 2012.

Waiting beside thee bail of straw
Shallow breezes softly gracing this face
Day time, mostly blue skies
With hints of funny shaped clouds
A fly lands on my shoulder, trembling in fear
Of its impending death or savour
Electric rays, signals, shooting through me like military lasers
Not causing problems as of now, but in time things will change
Believers of sin are flustered when the heavenly give to their fellow follower
Believers of the heavenly are sickened when the sinned take lives

The bail and I are still waiting in this field, for your return
Hours are going to convert to days
Bails may live, I well be eroded away like forgotten mountains
Pressure is mounting from peer, unwelcomed, stressors
Crunch, crunch, in the tall grasses from behind me
Could it be what were waiting for?
Turn around to see a women, appears to be in distress
Coming towards me at a calm pace
She kneels in front of my place in the grass
An whispers, are you the one waiting?
Yes, I'm waiting for there return, I speak

She stands up, puts her hands on my shoulders
Whispers, don't be scared it wont hurt for long
Flashes of light come from all sides of the day sky
Like a giant rainbow falling over on top of me
Falling on my back, seeing a star lit backdrop
Spinning in upward circles, strapped to an invisible vessel or table
Let lose to free fall through the star filled highway
Comets swimming by like electric fish
Am I ascending, descending, or from side to side
Suddenly a halt or pause thee has stopped
Still in a space of no recognizable formations

Its ice cold here just bobbing in crazy mindless black twilight oblivion
Alone no one or anything to strike a conversation with
Waiting once again, but for some sort of end
Madness, a dolphin approaches my spot out here
Underneath it comes up from, grabbing its fin
Taking off like a bullet, to out of mind speed
Crossing the night field in unusual fashion
Approaching a planet, covered mostly in blue

Colliding with the atmosphere, losing breath and senses
BANG, right through the blue, into underwater caverns
Still speeding like a mad fish, whiplash corners, angles

Light appearing ahead, straight out of the drink
Soaked body, hands slip off the fin
Falling straight back onto a bail of straw
Sunshine over head, waves crashing near by
I hear conversation, standing up feeling no pain
There are they, I've arrived to the what I was waiting for
A fly savour, a women in distress, straw bail transferred, dolphin rescued
I've just traveled the **GATE RAIL** Sunday, April 10, 2011.

Its Christmas eve, your at your families home, friends or else where
Out of the corner of your eye, you see a man dressed in a suit an tie
Surprise it's me, confronting me, you wonder to my presence
Maybe lock your door next time, just kidding other
means have brought me here tonight
In my hand I have an object, can you guess what it is?
You say, snow globe, I say close, it's a very special snow globe
Here shake it up an look into its magical snow scape

A snowflake lands on your head, two, then three, where are we? You say
Inside this special globe of snow, look outside the
plastic glass, see yourself holding it? I say
Don't be scared it's not cold here, nothing can hurt you, everything is friendly
Look around this small forest you will see only the people you love
Their faces flash like Christmas lights or lights in a night club
Off to the side of the trees, on plastic glass, that acts as a multi screen television
You will see all the places you've been and places you want to go
Look for a few minutes as I feed this reindeer, oh the clarity

Hop on the back of Rudolph here, we are going
for a ride to the center of your globe
Hold on we are heading for that vortex in the sky, it may be a bumpy ride
Through the rotating tunnel, you close your eyes and
hear your friends and families voices
They say, whispering you're almost there, just a little further
The tunnel stops spinning and just disappears, looking below you see a vast city
Lights shining up towards the heavens, a very
overwhelming feeling this place is giving you
You ask where are we? I say, I cannot reveal its name as
it's your globe, where do you think you are?

Rudolph lands at the center of this city, there is an
individual or being, twenty feet in front of you
This one person or spirit is at the center of your life, go up to them

People of the city form a circle around us, you may recognize
a few faces, all lights shine down towards you
As you walk to that individual or individuals, people of the city stop talking
I whisper, ask that being only one question and take their right hand
Taking their hand, they say, the answer will be in
your hand when mine leaves yours
Closing your eyes, seconds later you feel someone tap your shoulder
Your eyes open, right back in the Christmas eve where you started
In your hand a special snow globe, where all the
creatures an people look up to you
I wave and disappear, but wish you a very Merry Christmas and Happy New Year.

SNOW GLOBE

Sunday, December 22, 2013.

CONCLUSION

Its hard to believe to me anyway that it has taken 4 years to write an publish this book. If you are reading this I am forever grateful with your support on purchasing of Different Seconds Ten 2. Along this long road I have run into a lot of ups and downs, no matter the obstacle I kept on going to the end, you should remember that also for your goals and dreams! A great network of friends and family have supported me, with my writing for that I thank them, this book is because you and for you!

ACKNOWLEDGEMENTS

The reason there happens to be a second book is from overwhelming support from, family and friends. At one point or another during the creation of this book, you have either inspired an idea, said some positive words about my writing style, helped or have been there for me. For these reasons I dedicate this book to you, thank you very much!

Family:
Kim B., Chuck B., Dave A., Sheila W., Ron V., Carol V., Ryan V., Jennifer V., Christy P., John P., Kimberleigh P., Emily P., Andrew P., Krista K., Donna K., John K., Brittany K., Jordan K., Cassidy W., Scott W., Mary B., Ervin B., Adam B., Thomas B., Carol K., Sol K., Michael K., Jennifer K., Bryan K., Barb B., Jim., Matt B., Steve B., Shirley D.

Friends:
Lisa J., Alec J., Noah I., Vanessa I., Laura F., Laura G., Laura B., Alec H., Blake M., Adam M., Tim D., Ashley J., Ashley Hop., Ashley Hou., Laurie P., Joe R., Shawna R., Landon R., Wavey R., Josh T., Sarah T., Susan T., Nicole Ba., Nicole Bo., Gabriel H., Kara B., Kayla T., Amy C., Jon W., Stephie T., Krista E., Michele K., Christina S., Melissa T., Jill W., Catherine C., Rachel C., Caitlin M., Olivia M., Emily M., Nathan S., Shane M., April B., Jennifer R., Aliza R., Crystal P., Nicole D., Amanda G., Jennifer H., Sarah R., Kirstin S., Nathan S., Paul F., Brittany D., Brittany P., Chad M., Julie H., Joe C., Jan C., Josh M., Joanna Lm., Amber M., Amanda H., Katie C., Sandra C., Sandra B., Michelle W., Leslie C., Heather A., Sarah B., Alex B., Amy D., Tarah D., Marc J., Lisa H., Mackenzie KC., Leah M., Nabil M., Natalie P., Jenn S., Denise S., Julie S., Jeanene V., Bryan W., Matt W., Veronica W., Bobbi W., Tony P., Mallory W., Courtney T., Jasmine M., Daisy R., Debbie P., Jenn M., Jordan O., Goren W., Cullen S., Clayton R., Faye K., Sean M., Lisa L., Julie S., Josh B., Tyler A., Kam H.

Even if your name isn't listed, consider this book dedicated you regardless!

Cover photo:
Nathan Shirk, close left
Shane MacMillan, far left
Emily Munro, center looking out of the sunroof
Jonathan Wilkins, close right, couple
Amy Cuppage, close right, couple

Editing:
Lisa Judt, Editor

Photography:
Hilary Knegt Photography, both cover photo an author photo

Author name:
Josh and Sarah Trombley, through a group called college an careers, hosted by these two, the suggestion of my author name came to be! Thanks also for all the support from all involved with this group!

I would also like to dedicate this book to my late grandparents, Margaret Verrall an Ronald Verrall, may they rest in peace!

Along the way of writing poetry, I have got a pretty awesome fan base, I don't know all your names, or even where you are on this earth, but consider this book dedicated to you as well, thank you for your on going support, it's greatly appreciated!

CPSIA information can be obtained at www.ICGtesting.com
Printed in the USA
LVOW06s1913100614

389449LV00001B/8/P